8/74

−0032
.91
...at

55p

‑‑
0

20p

A Who's Who of Flapland

A Who's Who of Flapland
and other plays

DAVID HALLIWELL

FABER AND FABER
3 Queen Square
London

First published in 1971
by Faber and Faber Limited
3 Queen Square London WC1
Printed in Great Britain by
Latimer Trend & Co Ltd Plymouth
All rights reserved

ISBN 0 571 09674 3 (cloth bound)
ISBN 0 571 09678 6 (paper covers)

CONTENTS

A Who's Who of Flapland

First Man
Second Man

A Who's Who of Flapland was originally written for sound radio and was first broadcast on the BBC Third Programme on 22nd June 1967.

FIRST MAN   Alfred Marks
SECOND MAN   Wilfred Pickles

      Produced by Ronald Mason

A Who's Who of Flapland was first performed as theatre at the Green Banana on 13th November 1969 and was presented by Inter-Action.

FIRST MAN   Joe Melia
SECOND MAN   Walter Hall

      Directed by Naftali Yavin
      Stage Manager Peter Bourke

A self-service café. General background noise of conversation and crockery. A man sitting by himself. His thoughts may be tape recorded.

FIRST MAN: I know the feller I'm looking for, oh yes I know the man I'm after. I shall come across 'im and it could be anywhere, any time. I remember 'im. I remember everything about 'im, I couldn't forget. I wasn't the first, oh no, I wasn't the first, don't forget that. Yes, I'm not merely looking out for meself, it's not just a personal thing. I shall be the instrument for all those others stretching back, helpless now, bedridden, pleading for aid. In tracking this man down I'm a public benefactor. In ten years 'e can have gone through the population of a small town. There I was night porter, Palm Court Hotel, May 1960, Hull. 'E came, put 'is name in the book, Manson, false name, must 'ave been, but I couldn't know that, I couldn't know that then. Wormed 'is way into my confidence, gave me drinks in 'is room, talked about business. Come to Hull to buy corned beef, 2,000 boxes down on the quay. I've got a lot to settle with 'im. But I shan't forget 'is face. I'm on the lookout, I'm always on the lookout. I know 'e could pop up anywhere. I know that 'e could be anywhere, 'e could be 'ere. I must be aware. I am aware, oh yes. I'm sure of that, don't worry. Ten long years I've been on the lookout, I'll track 'im down. Yes, I'll find 'im. Oh me tea's gone cold. Get another. Yes, in a minute. 'Ow long 'ave I been 'ere? Oh so long. Well it—— Wish I 'ad something to read.

11

Ought to 'ave bought a paper. Not many in 'ere today. Wonder why. Just a few, dotted about. That old woman, seen 'er before, comes in 'ere a lot. That purple coat. Those two fellers talking, could be plumbers. Youngsters over there, long 'air, don't know they're born. Then a uniform, what is it? Anyway 'e couldn't—No, some sort of functionary. Then a business type, fat neck, then over there a very ordinary—what could 'e be? Salesman, traveller, quite smart, brief case. Reading. Guardian, is it? About my age. Yes.——My God! No! It can't be! Watch 'im. But it can't be. 'E's looking up as 'e turns a page—My God, yes, it is! It's 'im! Now be careful, watch closely. Mustn't be too. . . . That hat it could be. And that head. Both jaunty, yes. And of course 'e'll 'ave aged just like me. Not as much though. No, 'e's 'ad the best, I've 'ad the worst. Yes, yes, it's 'im all right. I recognize 'im. I knew I would when the time came. After all these years there 'e is in this cafe right in front of me. I knew it 'ad to 'appen. It could 'appen 'ere as well as anywhere. Why not? Well, well, there 'e sits and 'e doesn't know. 'Ow far am I away? Four tables, twenty feet. Just twenty feet between us. Twenty feet and ten years. Oh if 'e only knew what's going to hit him. 'E reads on absorbed, but 'e'll soon be absorbed with something else. I'll make myself felt. Well, this is it. Now. Yes. I must go over to 'im and make myself known. Yes. The look on 'is face, the shock. P'raps 'e'll try to bolt. Well, I'll block 'is way. I'll chase 'im, it'll be worth it just to see the expression on 'is face. This is it. Come on. Up I get. Move down there. One table, two—'asn't looked up, still oblivious. Nearly there. What'll 'e do? Almost . . .

Hallo.

SECOND MAN: Uh.

FIRST MAN: Doesn't realize. Take a second.

I said Hallo.

SECOND MAN: Oh.

FIRST MAN: Still doesn't. Jostle 'im a bit.

I think we've met before.

SECOND MAN: Er . . . no, I don't think so.

12

FIRST MAN: Pretendin'. Ought to 'ave expected it. Part of 'is trade. Watch the eyes. They'll give 'im away.

Yes, I think we 'ave.

SECOND MAN: Well, I'm sorry, I don't remember.

FIRST MAN: Not a flicker. P'raps 'e doesn't recognize me after all these years. That's possible.

It was quite a while ago.

SECOND MAN: Oh, well, in that case. But I'm sorry I don't.

FIRST MAN: No, 'e doesn't recognize me. But it's 'im all right.

No, well. I suppose you don't.

SECOND MAN: No, I'm sorry, but it completely eludes me.

FIRST MAN: I'll play 'im along then spring it. Be more satisfying that way.

Mind if I sit down for a bit?

SECOND MAN: No, not at all, please do.

FIRST MAN: Ta.

SECOND MAN: Well, when did I previously have the pleasure?

FIRST MAN: Oh . . . several years ago.

SECOND MAN: Oh, a long time. Well, where did we . . . I mean how exactly

FIRST MAN: Well, let's say I 'appened to be somewhere where you came.

SECOND MAN: Somewhere where I came?

FIRST MAN: 'E can still lay it on. Same voice. I mustn't let too much out too soon.

A'm hoping you might remember.

SECOND MAN: No, I'm sorry. Give me a few clues.

FIRST MAN: It was several years ago.

SECOND MAN: How many, two, three?

FIRST MAN: Nearer ten.

SECOND MAN: Ten. Oh, well, no wonder I can't remember.

FIRST MAN: Well, I can remember.

SECOND MAN: You must have a good memory.

FIRST MAN: Well, let's say certain faces stick in me mind's eye.

SECOND MAN: And mine's one of them.

FIRST MAN: I think I can say that.

SECOND MAN: Should I be flattered or insulted?

FIRST MAN: That all depends.

13

SECOND MAN: Depends on what?

FIRST MAN: Depends on . . . 'ow you view the circumstances of, well, what passed between us.

SECOND MAN: Oh, something passed between us.

FIRST MAN: Oh, yes, you can definitely say that.

SECOND MAN: It all sounds rather ominous.

FIRST MAN: Watch 'im when you say this.

It was.

Doesn't that ring any bells?

SECOND MAN: Oh. I'm afraid not, but it's becoming very intriguing.

FIRST MAN: Smiles amiably the bastard. Oh, 'e's composed.

Aye, well, A think you might find it interesting.

SECOND MAN: You make it sound very dramatic. I

FIRST MAN: It 'ad its moments. For me anyway.

SECOND MAN: Well, I'm fascinated to think that I could have had such an impact on somebody. And so long ago. It hardly fits in with the usual impression I leave. Moments of high drama ten years ago. I'm afraid I can't recall any moments of even moderate interest in, when would it be . . . ?

FIRST MAN: 1960.

SECOND MAN: Yes, 1960. Was it in the course of an inspection?

FIRST MAN: Well, I supp

SECOND MAN: Where was it?

FIRST MAN: You still don't remember?

SECOND MAN: No. Look, tell me.

FIRST MAN: All right, 'ere it is. I'll let 'im 'ave it. Both barrels. Watch 'is face.

All right.

SECOND MAN: Wait a jiff. Before you start. I could do with another tea. What about you?

FIRST MAN: 'E knows me! It's all been an act. 'E's going to bolt. Wait a minute!

SECOND MAN: What's the matter?

FIRST MAN: You can't just leave like this. I mean I want to tell you who I am.

SECOND MAN: Yes, yes, of course you do. I'm not going. I'm only going for another tea. I asked you if you wanted one.

14

FIRST MAN: Oh . . . well.

SECOND MAN: Can I get you a tea?

FIRST MAN: Oh . . . thanks.

SECOND MAN: Good. Back in a minute.

FIRST MAN: Watch him. If 'e tries to dash out the door after 'im.
Well, 'e's going towards the counter, turning round the end
of the rail, past the buns and biscuits, past the cooked
stuff

SECOND MAN: . . . I'm sure, I'm sure I've never set eyes on this
chap before. If we have met it must have been something
very casual. There's something a little disturbing about
him. Look at him now, out of the corner of my eye.
Watching every move I make. I wonder
Two teas, please.
I wonder who he thinks I am? Perhaps he's mistaken me
for somebody else. Yes, that could be it. He seems to
attach great significance to
Thank you.
Ah well, I'll get back and find out what he's talking about.

FIRST MAN: 'E's paying. . . . Putting change in 'is pocket.
Coming back. Does 'e look apprehensive? No cool as a
cucumber balancing the teas. Smooth as ever. Here 'e
comes.

SECOND MAN: Here we are.

FIRST MAN: Ta.

SECOND MAN: Good. Now you were just on the point of eluci-
dating the mystery of our past encounter.

FIRST MAN: Yes.

SECOND MAN: Oh, I only brought one spoon.

FIRST MAN: 'Ere, you can 'ave this.

SECOND MAN: Thanks. No point in going back for another.

FIRST MAN: No.

SECOND MAN: Well, where, when and how?

(*Short pause.*)

FIRST MAN: I am Victor Peddy!

SECOND MAN: Oh . . . are you? Well, I'm Frank Thornton.
Pleased to meet you. Or I suppose I should say pleased to
meet you again.

FIRST MAN: My name doesn't mean anything to you?

SECOND MAN: No, sorry, 'fraid not.

FIRST MAN: Well, it soon will.

SECOND MAN: I shall be only too pleased if it does.

FIRST MAN: When I add a few choice details.

SECOND MAN: Ah, nothing like the hand-picked detail.

FIRST MAN: Such as time and place.

SECOND MAN: Yes, they'd make a neat start.

FIRST MAN: Oh, yes.

SECOND MAN: Well, go ahead.

FIRST MAN: May 1960, Hull, Palm Court Hotel, Night Porter. Cubby-'ole under the stairs, corned beef, 2,000 boxes!

SECOND MAN: Two thousand boxes of corned beef in a cubbyhole under the stairs!

FIRST MAN: So you still deny it?

SECOND MAN: Of course I deny *it*. I don't even know what you mean by *it*.

FIRST MAN: Very clever but the game's up.

SECOND MAN: Look, if you think I'm somebody you met in Hull in what is it, 1960, I can assure you you're completely mistaken.

FIRST MAN: Oh, come off it, Manson, the game's up. There's no need to go on bluffing!

SECOND MAN: What did you call me?

FIRST MAN: Manson.

SECOND MAN: But my name's Thornton, I told you.

FIRST MAN: I knew you as Manson.

SECOND MAN: You certainly did not.

FIRST MAN: You know very well what I'm talking about. May '60, Palm Court, Hull. I was there, the night porter. You came there, you wore a charcoal grey coat and a dark hat. You 'ad a case, what d' they call it, a sample case. Every night you came in about midnight. Every night for six days. Always when I was on duty. You picked your time. You struck up an acquaintance with me, talked about the racing, talked about the decline in the fishing industry. You invited me up to your room for drinks, 307, fifth floor. You got yourself into my confidence, patted me on my

16

back, said you couldn't understand what a man like me was doing as a night porter. You told me all about your business, 'ow you were in Hull on behalf of your partners in Manchester. The men with steely hearts you called 'em. That's 'ow you phrased it. I remember that phrase because it was you who 'ad the steely heart. You told me you were there to snap up the corned beef stacked in a ware'ouse on the quay. You said you 'ad £250 in cash to clinch the deal, and another £1,750 in the bank, the Manchester branch, to cover the balance on delivery. You showed me the £250, in the case. "Look," you said, and snapped it open. "Look, this's it," you said. £250 quid all in tenners. It looked real, I thought it looked real, it must 'ave been theatrical. But 'ow was I to know, I'd never seen a tenner before, I've never seen one since. "Into my wallet", you said, "and down to the dock tomorra morning to get the corned beef, cash on the nail," you said, "the rest later. In twenty-four hours the lorries will be rolling west, through the Pennines and down into Manchester." It sounded like an idyll. It made me envious. We drank to it. To all the fat profit you and your partners were going to make. Then the next day, next night, to be exact, I'd just come on, just after nine, you knew that, you'd timed it with a stop-watch, nothing left to chance with a man like you. In you came urgent and flushed into the lobby. I was behind the reception desk. I was looking through the reception book, that's what a night porter 'ad to do. Up you came and "Can I 'ave a private word?" you said. "Vic," you said, "very important, Vic." Well, we couldn't go into the dining-room because they were dining, we couldn't go into the lounge because they were—lounging. We couldn't stay in the lobby because they were moving up and down all the time. We couldn't go up to your room because I couldn't go out of the sound of the bell, the bell on the desk, it was a busy time, nine. So the only place left was the closet, the cubby-'ole under the stairs. We 'ad to squeeze in there. You can't 'ave forgotten that, we couldn't stand up, we couldn't turn round. I was pushed right in, into the angle, I was bent over on meself like a sandwich. You can't 'ave finalized all your schemes in such restricted places. But you finalized me all right. Yes, Mr. Manson, you finalized me good an' proper, I've been a has-been ever since. You told me you'd lost the wallet, lost the deposit, you told me you'd been running round Hull all day trying to find it. You said you 'ad to 'ave the cash or the corned beef would go elsewhere, the lorries would be rolling in some other direction. And if they did your pals would have your hide! They'd never let you live it down. So I 'and over my savings, £246 to the penny. The scrapings of three years, what I'd gleaned together to give meself another chance after the bust up with the Chinese crowd—which you know all about. Oh, yes, you made it sound all above board, in return for my savings I'd get a document signing over all your profits on the deal to me, all the profits in your name, the steely men in Manchester wouldn't ever know. So you got my money and I got your scrap of paper, written in biro, green biro. Off you go and that's the last I ever clapped eyes on you. Though a day 'asn't gone by when I 'aven't been looking, on the streets, the buses, the cafés, the foyers, the stations. The corned beef! Oh, that was there all right. I went down there, it was there all right, 3,000 boxes not 2,000, p'raps that's something you don't know. There it all was. Property of Mr. Harry Leiberman! Manson? They'd never 'eard of 'im. Who was 'e? When I showed 'em the document, scribbled in green biro, they couldn't control their faces, they didn't even try, they escorted me to the exit! So that's what we've 'ad to do with one another, that's 'ow we met before, that's why I've never forgotten your face. You've cost me £246, ten years in sleep, an' all the chance I ever 'ad of ever making out in business.

(*Pause.*)

SECOND MAN: Well, that's quite a story. But I'm afraid you're making a big mistake.

FIRST MAN: I'm making no mistake. What are you trying to say, I invented all this?

18

SECOND MAN: No, I'm not saying that. All I'm saying is that I'm not the man you think. I'm not the one who did it all to you.

FIRST MAN: I know you're 'im.

SECOND MAN: How can you be so sure?

FIRST MAN: 'Is face is engraved on the back of my eyes.

SECOND MAN: The memory gets distorted after such a long period.

FIRST MAN: Mine doesn't. Not about this.

SECOND MAN: Well, apart from this memory of a face

FIRST MAN: I remember the tilt of 'is 'ead.

SECOND MAN: Yes, okay, but apart from these physical characteristics, what other proof, what other means of identification have you got?

FIRST MAN: What more do I want?

SECOND MAN: A lot more. Photographs

FIRST MAN: You don't think a man like that would let 'imself get photographed with a budding victim.

SECOND MAN: I suppose not. But what about this document you talk about? I suppose you've kept that?

FIRST MAN: I threw it away in disgust. Into the sea.

SECOND MAN: That was rash.

FIRST MAN: What good would it 'ave been? You don't think 'e— I mean I know that you didn't sign it with a real name. I knew Manson's no more your name than Thornley is.

SECOND MAN: I said Thornton.

FIRST MAN: What does it matter, they're all false names.

SECOND MAN: The name on the paper doesn't matter, but the handwriting would. I mean you could check my writing with the writing on the document.

FIRST MAN: You think you're being very clever. But I've learnt a lot since we met before. I know you can change the way you write as easily as—I can change me shirt.

SECOND MAN: You don't appear to find that too easy.

FIRST MAN: What?

SECOND MAN: Let it go. This man would have to be a master forger to change his handwriting at will.

FIRST MAN: Well, you are, I know that.

19

SECOND MAN: How could you know that?

FIRST MAN: The money in the case, the tenners, all forged.

SECOND MAN: How do you know it was?

FIRST MAN: It must 'ave been. 'E wouldn't carry real money, real tenners, where would 'e get it?

SECOND MAN: From a bank presumably. But you wouldn't know whether it was real or not, you said so yourself.

FIRST MAN: Still as cocky as ever. Still think you're ten times smarter than anybody else. Well, I don't 'ave to

SECOND MAN: Look, the only thing that I know is that I'm not the man you're looking for. In the first place I wasn't in Hull in 1960, either in the month of May or in the month of anything else.

FIRST MAN: Then where d'you claim you were?

SECOND MAN: I thought you'd ask me that. Mmm's not an easy one to answer.

FIRST MAN: Ah, so you can't tell me!

SECOND MAN: I didn't say I couldn't tell you, I said it wouldn't be easy. I lack your gift for instant reminiscences dating so far back. Now let me see, 1960. Ten years ago. Mm— got married in . . . How long have we

FIRST MAN (*as* SECOND MAN *continues*): Look, I'm not

SECOND MAN: I listened to you so be good enough to listen to me.

FIRST MAN: Oh!

SECOND MAN: Where was I . . . you see you've broken the . . . ah, I got married in '57. I'd been married a few months when they sent me to Gateshead, it was cold, it was winter. Then in June, yes, the following June, June '58. I was moved to Head Office. I was there until the replacement came and that was well into 1959. He came, yes, he came, little chap, face like a gorilla, no shoulders, asthmatic, I should think. He came and then the travels began. They sent me . . . Southampton, Liverpool, Manchester . . . don't jump to any conclusions I didn't ally myself with any steely-hearted gentleman whilst I was there—Liverpool, Manchester, Kendal, London. Yes, those were the . . . But which came when? What's the order? The first one was the farthest. Yep. So I went to Southampton. When was I there? Summer, yes, warm weather. Oh, yes, the girl with nothing on, I remember her. Then they shunted me to Manchester. No, Liverpool. Ah, yes, one port to another. The ferry, very sharp wind, so I was there next winter. Winter '59–'60. So I arrived at the beginning of the year in question. Now when did I . . . Yes, Kendal, Lake District, I was on my own up there, magnificent scenery. And after that they sent me to London. Yes, but when? Before May?

FIRST MAN: Oh, this's getting nowhere. I don't want to listen to all this. I've never 'eard anything so fantastic. I know where you were. I don't believe a word of it. Girls with nothing on, men with no shoulders, what do you think I am? You can't get out of it with all this, you can't

SECOND MAN: Oh, yes, it is getting us somewhere, it's getting me somewhere anyway. It's got me to the year in question.

FIRST MAN: Oh.

SECOND MAN: Please. Now I know where I was, I was in Kendal. Yes, in May '60 I was up in the Lakes. Now let's see if I can narrow it down. See if I can remember exactly what I was doing. Amazing what you can remember when you get down to it. Well . . . I was on the job, yes, out in the car every day. And I was staying? Let me see . . . I stayed in two places up there. The first place was . . . Mrs. Shane's, Shanelly, what was her . . . ? Never mind. Oh yes, she was the one I christened the W.C. Watcher, very unpleasant, got out of there pretty niftily. Moved to a hotel, all expenses paid. Yes, so it didn't matter. Worth paying for a bit of peace and quiet. What was the place called? Had a sign. Ornate sort of thing with arms and all that. Arms, yes . . . and a crown. Ah, yes, the King . . . King William. Now, there was a yellow carpet in the hall, or lobby, as you'd say

FIRST MAN: I wou

SECOND MAN: brown oak panelling and . . . Wait a minute! The porter!

FIRST MAN: What's

SECOND MAN: I know who you are! Good gracious! We have

met before and it was in May 1960. But it wasn't at the Palm Court in Hull, it was at the King William in Kendal.

FIRST MAN: Now

SECOND MAN: And you weren't the night porter, you were the day porter.

FIRST MAN: Don't be bloody stupid. I've never been there. You were

SECOND MAN: Well, of all the . . . ! You know I thought there was something vaguely familiar about you. It was just a vague sensation at the back of my mind

FIRST MAN: What are you trying

SECOND MAN: that's why I listened to you, I suppose. When you told me all about Hull I thought I must be wrong, I must be confusing him with someone else a little like him, but I couldn't put my finger on anyone tangible. And of course you've aged. But now I recognize you. Oh, yes, it's all flooding back.

FIRST MAN: What are you tryin' to pull now? You can't

SECOND MAN: Oh, yes, I can—Mr. P. Wood.

FIRST MAN: My name's Peddy and I was in Hull.

SECOND MAN: Your name was Wood and you were in Kendal.

FIRST MAN: Come off it, Manson. Very clever, but it won't

SECOND MAN: The name's Thornton.

FIRST MAN: It's Manson and I'm Peddy.

SECOND MAN: It's Wood and I'm Thornton.

FIRST MAN: It's Manson and

SECOND MAN: Bandying names won't get us very far. Call yourself whatever you like for the moment it doesn't matter. Yes, I recall you standing at your post, erect and soldierly, my how it all comes back to me. There you were standing sentinel just in front of the little flap of the reception desk. That's right. Now one had to go through that flap to reach the little door which led into the little dell at the back of the building. I always thought what bad planning. But you delighted in that flap, it was almost your *raison d'être,* your surface *raison d'être* at any rate.

FIRST MAN: I don't know what you're talking about.

SECOND MAN: Before one could exit into the garden, if you can call it a garden, let's call it a dell for the time being. Before one could gain access to that secluded spot, one had to request you to flip up your flap. And you executed that service with a precision and dignity worthy of a State Funeral. Clipped turn, clipped flip, clipped salute. Did you ever refuse to let anyone through and if so on what grounds?

FIRST MAN: I

SECOND MAN: Merely rhetorical. Haha, yes, you were very impressive. Oh, yes. And the false eye. Good gracious. That's why it took the penny so long to drop. You led me to believe that you had a glass eye.

FIRST MAN: Don't be

SECOND MAN: Oh, yes, you did. And I did believe you. I would have sworn blind—rather apt—I would have sworn blind if anyone had asked me in those days, that one of your eyes was a glass one.

FIRST MAN: I've never

SECOND MAN: Which one did you say it was? The left, yes. It just shows what the power of suggestion can do. I accepted it completely. I must have looked into your eyes a thousand times and I always thought that one of them returned a glassy insensitive stare. And yet now I look into them and there's no question but that they're both as gelatinous as could be. You haven't got a glass eye and you never had.

FIRST MAN: My eyes 'ave always been real.

SECOND MAN: I accept it without question. But it just goes to show what powers of suggestion you commanded in those faraway days. And it's the reason I never connected you in the first place with P. Wood of perfidious memory who so thoroughly took me to the cleaners as they say in one of the towns I've passed through on life's road—Which one? Brighouse probably—But never mind. And so, you see, it was the eye that threw me.

FIRST MAN: You're the man

SECOND MAN: I am the man who was taken in by the day porter at the King William Hotel, Kendal.

FIRST MAN: That's not the truth. You're the confidence trickster.

23

SECOND MAN: No, it's the other way about.

FIRST MAN: That's absurd. You can't

SECOND MAN: The little pool, eh? The little pool out in the back, in the dell.

FIRST MAN: What are y' talkin' about?

SECOND MAN: Oh, stop pretending. Come out into the open. I'm admiring your ability, can't you see that? I'm on the point of paying tribute to the magnificent ease and breathtaking panache with which you acquitted your part of the exercise. Why the whole movement of it together with my inadvertent countermovements under your deft direction had the grace and timing of a minuet. You were an artist in those days.

FIRST MAN: Oh.

SECOND MAN: Ah, I can see that your proper sense of professional pride is enticing you out of mufti.

FIRST MAN: Well

SECOND MAN: Yes, I can see

FIRST MAN: I 'aven't admitted anything.

SECOND MAN: Are you sure?

FIRST MAN: Of course I'm sure. Anyway, what is all this? What are you gettin' at?

SECOND MAN: I'm rather reverently referring to a simple transaction enacted near the shores of England's largest inland water.

FIRST MAN: What's that supposed to mean?

SECOND MAN: I can see you want to hear all the details of your impeccable manœuvre recounted by the victim. Yes, that will be doubly satisfying for you.

FIRST MAN: Er

SECOND MAN: Well, here goes. You went out of your way to strike up conversation with me. And the conversation often turned to fishing. Now I knew nothing about fishing and you obviously guessed that. But your dissertations on fishing fascinated me. Before I knew it you were enticing me through your flap with full military honours to view the dell. And of course once in the dell I was bound to notice the pool. Not because I'm particularly observant,

24

I'm not, but even I couldn't avoid noticing that scoop of water because of its smell. At first I thought to myself, that must be the smell of real country water, that's the smell of the real outdoor water, mustn't allow my decadent urban nostrils to blench from it. It's raw but it's healthy, brace up and re-embrace Mother Nature, back to the roots and so on. It was only in retrospect that I discovered that our little pond was the hotel sump. However, you told me that you had purchased the fishing concession from the manageress and you were going to stock it with trout. You were going to buy 400 quidsworth of trout and put them in the pool. Ideal that pool for trout, you said. You were the expert. Once the pool was replete with trout the guests of the King William were to be allowed to fish out their own dinners at two quid a time. An added amenity for the hotel and a nice little sideline for you, Mr. Wood. And for me, too, if I was interested. You were looking for a partner to put up half the cash. Oh, don't you revel as much as I do in the memory of that visit we paid to the hatcheries? All those spry little fishes darting about in their tanks. Well, to cut a long story rather shorter, I handed over the lolly and the next morning you were gone from your post. The flap lay open and unguarded. A brief word with the manageress and I knew the awful truth. No trout could last five seconds in the pool without respirator. She knew it, you knew it, and I finally knew it too. But now we've met again and to put it bluntly you owe me 200 quid!

FIRST MAN: Now wait a minute.

SECOND MAN: I realize you haven't got it on you.

FIRST MAN: I don't owe you anything.

SECOND MAN: Oh, well, if you're going to be like that about it. I was prepared to be lenient, let you off with, say, a hundred. After all it was a long time ago and you pulled it off so well. I have a sneaking admiration and all that. But if you're going to be awkward

FIRST MAN: I'm not being awkward. It's you who's being

SECOND MAN: You conned me for 200 smackers. Now come on.

FIRST MAN: I wasn't there. I was in Hull.

SECOND MAN: You were in Kendal. Now come on.

FIRST MAN: I'm off. You're barmy. I'm not

SECOND MAN: Sit down.

FIRST MAN: No, I'll let it go. I'll let it

SECOND MAN: I think you'd better sit down. If you leave this café, I shall be right behind you. You can't run faster than I can. I'm fitter than you. Sit down.

FIRST MAN: What for?

SECOND MAN: Perhaps we can come to some arrangement.

FIRST MAN: What kind of arrangement?

SECOND MAN: Sit down.

FIRST MAN: Oh . . . well . . . What is it y're

SECOND MAN: Good.

FIRST MAN: Now what is you're . . . A mean

SECOND MAN: You still maintain that you were in Hull?

FIRST MAN: Yes, yes, 'course I do.

SECOND MAN: And that I was there, too?

FIRST MAN: Well . . . er . . . now wait a bit, 'ang on. I think I can see what's 'appened. Y'see I was in Hull, no doubt about that, but what's 'appened is that I've mistaken you for somebody else. Somebody who looked very much like you.

SECOND MAN: So you'll accept that I was in Kendal?

FIRST MAN: Yes, yes, I do now. A mean the story you tell, it's very convincin'.

SECOND MAN: But if I was in Kendal, what about my remembering you as being there too?

FIRST MAN: Well, can't you see what's 'appened? The same thing. There must 'ave been a bloke very much like me there. Just as there was one very much like you where I was. I mean 'e looked like you, the temperament was obviously diff'rent. The same thing 'appened in both places. That's 'ow all this confusion came about.

SECOND MAN: I see. So what you're saying is that there are two men in the world, or were at the time we're speaking of, one who is the spitting image of me and one who is the spitting image of yourself.

FIRST MAN: Yes, that's it.

SECOND MAN: Amazing.

FIRST MAN: Aye, but there it is.

SECOND MAN: It sends an eerie shiver down my spine to think that there are these other two men, Wood and Manson, looking for all the world like you and me, sneaking about the country, perpetrating the most cunning frauds whilst we innocently go about our business.

FIRST MAN: Aye, it's not a pleasant thought.

SECOND MAN: I wonder whether they've ever bumped into one another?

FIRST MAN: Well, I don't know.

SECOND MAN: Well, it's not beyond the bounds of possibility. After all, we know they both travel round a great deal. I mean the nature of their profession demands it.

FIRST MAN: Well, A suppose it's possible.

SECOND MAN: Why they could be sitting in some quiet café at this very minute. Talking. And if they are, I have a very shrewd idea what the topic will be.

FIRST MAN: What?

SECOND MAN: Our good selves.

FIRST MAN: Well, I don't see that.

SECOND MAN: But it's obvious, my dear chap. Manson on seeing Wood would take him for you. Whilst Wood on seeing Manson would take him for me.

FIRST MAN: Oh, I shall find that man one of these days and when I do, I'll

SECOND MAN: How will you know it's him?

FIRST MAN: I shall know. 'Is face is engraved on my mind.

SECOND MAN: But you mistook me for him.

FIRST MAN: Ah yes, but that was a mistake.

SECOND MAN: You've discerned that I, perhaps only in some minor way, am not exactly like him? I mean they say that no two human beings are ever exactly alike.

FIRST MAN: Yes, yes, now I know who you are, I can see there are diff'rences.

SECOND MAN: For instance?

FIRST MAN: Well . . . to begin with, Manson 'ad a little mole just under 'is chin. Very little but it was there.

27

SECOND MAN: Go on.

FIRST MAN: Well, then again 'e 'ad a bit less 'air than you've got.

SECOND MAN: What else?

FIRST MAN: Well, the 'air was a diff'rent shade. More reddy coloured.

SECOND MAN: Mine's not red at all.

FIRST MAN: No, of course, it isn't. But 'is was. Oh, yes, you couldn't miss it, A mean if you really looked, and I did, I 'ad good opportunities especially in that closet.

SECOND MAN: Anything else?

FIRST MAN: Yes, 'is face, it was a bit fatter. 'E 'ad chubby cheeks. 'Is face was rounder.

SECOND MAN: Is that all?

FIRST MAN: Oh, no. A mean now that A look at you, the tilt of the head, 'e 'eld it more forward, you 'old it more backward. Then the shoulders, 'is weren't as wide, 'e 'ad narrer shoulders, yours are broad. And you're quite a shade taller. In fact 'e was shorter, smallish really, not a dwarf, but a little man. 'E 'ad a snubby nose, yours is pointed, 'is eyes were close set, yours are wide.

SECOND MAN: How very strange.

FIRST MAN: Oh, it's not strange. It was an accident of the light. You've got a similar kind of coat on, that's 'ow I mistook you. Y're nothing like 'im.

SECOND MAN: But as I say it's strange.

FIRST MAN: Why?

SECOND MAN: Because I am him.

FIRST MAN: What!

SECOND MAN: I said I am him.

FIRST MAN: But

SECOND MAN: I am the man you took me for at first. The man you knew as Manson.

FIRST MAN: That's impossible! You can't be!

SECOND MAN: Yes, I'm afraid I am. Palm Court Hotel.

FIRST MAN: But this is

SECOND MAN: Please hear me out. Palm Court Hotel, Hull, May 1960, yes, I was there. As soon as you sat down I recognized you. I'm glad this has happened. I've been harrowed by what I did to you all those years ago. And by all the others, widows, cripples, bargees, a female psychiatrist from Finland. My conscience has never given me a moment's rest. I'm relieved that one of my victims has had the stamina and acuity to track me down and run me to earth. I'm tired and weary, I crave release. The release that only the catharsis of punishment can bring. I confess everything. The corned beef, the counterfeit money—they were fivers by the way, not tenners—the hard men in Manchester, the document written in biro. Yes, it's all only too true. Please call the police. I shan't run away, I'm tired of running, go ahead, turn me in, I'll tell them everything.

FIRST MAN: But, no! This's . . . You can't be!

SECOND MAN: Yes, I am. You can call the police from here. They'll have a phone.

FIRST MAN: No, I

SECOND MAN: Oh, I know, you suspect a trick, you think that whilst I'm out of your sight I'll do a bunk. Don't worry. Call one of the girls over from the counter, tell her to make the call.

FIRST MAN: Now look, I don't

SECOND MAN: Or we can both go to the phone together.

FIRST MAN: No, no, I don't

SECOND MAN: Ah, You're getting up. I understand. You want to take me to the nearest police station in person. Very understandable. The satisfaction will be greater. Well, let's get it over with. After you.

FIRST MAN: No, no . . . Sit down.

SECOND MAN: No, come on. I've had enough. The time's come.

FIRST MAN: No, you don't understand, I er . . . I don't want to.

SECOND MAN: After all these years of looking for me. Of course you want to.

FIRST MAN: Yes, well I did, yes, but now I don't.

SECOND MAN: Your generosity of heart does you credit. But it's misplaced. I don't want leniency, I want to be punished.

FIRST MAN: No, no, you don't understand.

SECOND MAN: No, it's you who don't, I want you to arrest me. Please turn me in.

29

FIRST MAN: No, look, sit down.

SECOND MAN: Very well, if you aren't prepared to turn me in, I must turn myself in.

FIRST MAN: No, don't do that, please

SECOND MAN: Yes, I'll call one of those girls over.

FIRST MAN: No. You mustn't. There's been a mistake. Sit

SECOND MAN: How can there have been a mistake?

FIRST MAN: Er, I don't know but please

SECOND MAN: I know who I am.

FIRST MAN: Yeh, of course, but sit down, get back down.

SECOND MAN: But what's the point? I did you a great injustice and

FIRST MAN: Look, please sit down. Just give me a minute.

SECOND MAN: Oh very well. But let's not drag this out.

FIRST MAN: Aah. Now look, what you say, y' can't 'ave

SECOND MAN: Of course I did. Ten years ago in Hull.

FIRST MAN: No, no, it's not true.

SECOND MAN: Not true?

FIRST MAN: I wasn't there! I wasn't there in Hull.

SECOND MAN: Of course you were. You're the only man of your description I've ever met.

FIRST MAN: All right, you've met me 'ere, in 'ere, now. But before this other time, ten years ago, it was somebody else.

SECOND MAN: I couldn't possibly confuse you with anyone else.

FIRST MAN: I wasn't there.

SECOND MAN: If you weren't there, how is it you know everything about it and in such detail?

FIRST MAN: I was told about it.

SECOND MAN: Who told you about it?

FIRST MAN: A guest. A guest 'o was there at the same time it 'appened.

SECOND MAN: But how would a guest know about it?

FIRST MAN: 'E was told. Afterwards.

SECOND MAN: And who told him?

FIRST MAN: The man. The one you took in. Peddy.

SECOND MAN: Ah so now you claim your name isn't Peddy.

FIRST MAN: No, it's not.

SECOND MAN: Well, what do you claim it is now?

FIRST MAN: Galloway.

SECOND MAN: You expect me to believe that?

FIRST MAN: You've got t'believe it. It's me name.

SECOND MAN: Well, let's suppose just for the sake of argument
your name is—Galloway. Why did you pass yourself off as
Peddy?

FIRST MAN: Ah well, y'see, it's a bit complicated. Y'see, I knew
about Peddy as I say from this guest. I knew all about 'is . . .
spot o' trouble 'e'd 'ad, with you, in Hull. Now the reason I
knew, the reason, this guest told me all about it, the way
it came up in conversation was because I'd 'ad a similar
experience meself. Not in '60, sometime after, '62, with a
man 'o passed 'imself off as Ormeroyde. Now when I saw
you sittin' there I thought to meself. That looks like this
Manson feller 'o pulled the corned beef caper in Hull. I
thought, a day's going to come when I'm actually face to
face with Ormeroyde 'imself, A mean the law of averages
makes it unavoidable. And when that time comes I'll 'ave
to know the ropes, I'll 'ave to 'ave the perfect technique
for interrogatin' 'im. 'E's very slippery is Ormeroyde and
I'll 'ave to be on top to nail 'im. So I thought 'ere's a
marvellous chance to practise me technique, y'know,
actually in the field as they say. 'Ere in the flesh, unless
I've been given a bum description, is one of the greatest
living confidence tricksters of our time and if I pass meself
off as one of 'is past victims, Peddy, 'o's story I know by
'eart, I can see how I show up. I knew y'd tumble to me
sooner or later but A kept up the pretence as long as A
could. But I thought when 'e does tumble we'll 'ave a laugh
at it. I knew you were a man as appreciated a good laugh.
A mean, that'd been included in the description I'd been
given.

SECOND MAN: So this is the moment, according to you, when
we should commence guffawing.

FIRST MAN: Aye, yes, haha. I know 'o you are and you know 'o
I am.

SECOND MAN: Galloway, not Peddy.

FIRST MAN: That's it.

31

SECOND MAN: But if this is true, how is it that you exactly fit the description of the man in Hull?

FIRST MAN: Oh well, that must be the old memory playin' you tricks. Tricky thing the memory.

SECOND MAN: My memory doesn't play me tricks. Couldn't succeed in my business if it did. I could get caught out any time if I didn't keep the images for ever green of all those I've had professional dealings with in the past.

FIRST MAN: Well, it must be the power of suggestion then. I mean the power of my suggestion that I was Peddy that's what's done it. I mean all the details that I knew.

SECOND MAN: Well, even allowing for that to be so. How is it that after the power of your suggestion has spent itself, and even after I've listened to you, yourself, demolish the idea that you are Peddy. How is it that after all this you still resemble, in my eyes, down to the last minutiae, the man I knew as Peddy.

FIRST MAN: Well, I don't know. P'raps I look a bit like 'im.

SECOND MAN: My dear man, it's a good deal more than a passing visual similarity. You're in every way identical. You even smell like him.

FIRST MAN: What?

SECOND MAN: Oh, no offence intended. It's not in itself a bad odour. In fact it's rather pleasing.

FIRST MAN: Oh.

SECOND MAN: He was exactly like you. Even down to the way you stir your tea with your poison finger.

FIRST MAN: Eh?

SECOND MAN: I mean the degree of similarity it implies is only to be found amongst identical twins.

FIRST MAN: Well.

SECOND MAN: You don't happen to have a twin, do you?

FIRST MAN: Ah. That's it! Y've put your finger on it. Why didn't I think of it before!

SECOND MAN: You mean you have a twin?

FIRST MAN: Yes, yes I mean I 'ad. Oh, I 'aven't thought about it in years. That's why A didn't mention it before. I'd completely forgotten about it. It's so long since I saw 'im.

32

SECOND MAN: Well, where is this twin? What does he do?

FIRST MAN: Oh now, there y've got me. Y'see I 'aven't seen 'im since we were kids. I 'aven't seen 'im since 'e was five.

SECOND MAN: How come?

FIRST MAN: Well, 'e ran away from 'ome.

SECOND MAN: When he was five?

FIRST MAN: Aye. That's why I can 'ardly remember 'im.

SECOND MAN: It seems a rather early age to strike out for oneself.

FIRST MAN: It is. It was.

SECOND MAN: Oh, come come, do you expect me to believe that a child of five ran away and disappeared. How could a child of that age survive on its own?

FIRST MAN: Ah well, y'see, 'e ran away to an orphanage.

SECOND MAN: How do you know that?

FIRST MAN: Me father, a workmate of 'is told 'im.

SECOND MAN: How did the workmate know?

FIRST MAN: Well 'e did a spare-time job at the orphanage.

SECOND MAN: What was it?

FIRST MAN: Oh, I don't know, I forget now. I think 'e entertained.

SECOND MAN: And when he told your father that his missing son, half the full set so to speak, was masquerading as a parentless waif, why didn't your father go and put an end to the charade?

FIRST MAN: Well like, me father, as far as I c'n remember, 'ad 'ad a diff'rence of opinion with me brother.

SECOND MAN: Over what?

FIRST MAN: Oh, I can't remember. A mean I was only a toddler at the time.

SECOND MAN: So was your brother.

FIRST MAN: Ah yeh, but 'e was more forward than me.

SECOND MAN: But you can't recall what issues separated father and son.

FIRST MAN: No, no, not off'and.

SECOND MAN: Foreign Affairs perhaps?

FIRST MAN: No, A don't think it was that.

SECOND MAN: But can you be absolutely sure?

FIRST MAN: Well, not absolutely, but it doesn't seem

SECOND MAN: I mean is it beyond the bounds of possibility that they differed, let us say, over the German Question?

FIRST MAN: No, my brother. I mean I don't think 'e

SECOND MAN: But why do you reject the possibility?

FIRST MAN: Well, I don't think 'e could read.

SECOND MAN: How do you know he couldn't?

FIRST MAN: Well, A never saw 'im. And I couldn't read.

SECOND MAN: But he was more advanced than you were.

FIRST MAN: That's true. But I never saw 'im read.

SECOND MAN: Perhaps he was a secret reader.

FIRST MAN: Well, A suppose 'e could 'ave been.

SECOND MAN: And if he was, what more natural than that in perusing some newspaper he should come upon the German Question?

FIRST MAN: Well, I suppose so.

SECOND MAN: And then some time later, whilst in casual conversation with his father, isn't it likely that he would touch upon what he'd read probably essaying the views he'd formed thereby, and isn't it even more likely that he would discover, to his shock perhaps, that his father was a polemicist of the opposite camp?

FIRST MAN: No, I don't think it can 'ave been. . . . Y'see, me father wasn't interested in that sort of thing.

SECOND MAN: You're certain of that?

FIRST MAN: Oh yes, definite.

SECOND MAN: Then it must have been something else.

FIRST MAN: Aye yes, y'see, me father, 'e was more a member of the old school. 'E couldn't read for a start. And A mean there was no secret about that. Ev'rybody knew. And that —ah yes, now A come to think of it—that's the reason— oh, it's all comin' back to me now, it's like you said, once y' start t' delve back—Aye, me father couldn't read and me brother could and that was it. That's where the friction was. And that's why Dermot, that was me brother's name, that's why Dermot ran away and that's why me father didn't want 'im back.

SECOND MAN: I see. And you've never set eyes on Dermot since?

FIRST MAN: Not once.

SECOND MAN: But you think that he was Victor Peddy?

FIRST MAN: Well, it seems the most likely explanation t'me, A mean 'e looked like me the last time I saw 'im, even our parents made mistakes, and I see no reason why 'e shouldn't 'ave gone on lookin' like me.

SECOND MAN: So Victor Peddy was really Dermot Galloway?

FIRST MAN: Must 'ave been.

SECOND MAN: He was the man in Hull.

FIRST MAN: It's obvious.

SECOND MAN: Who was the man in Kendal, then?

FIRST MAN: Eh?

SECOND MAN: Who was the man in Kendal who also resembled you?

FIRST MAN: But you

SECOND MAN: You're not a triplet by any chance?

FIRST MAN: Now wait a minute, you said you made 'im up.

SECOND MAN: I was lying.

FIRST MAN: But I don't get it. I mean if you were

SECOND MAN: The story I told you about Kendal was true in every detail.

FIRST MAN. But you said you were there the same time I said . . . I mean what about Hull?

SECOND MAN: I was in Kendal, your brother was in Hull.

FIRST MAN: But you admitted you were in Hull too. That's 'ow you met 'im.

SECOND MAN: That was a lie. I was in Kendal.

FIRST MAN: But why? I mean

SECOND MAN: So I could get you to admit that you weren't in Hull. Thus leaving yourself free time and space to confess without any implausibility that you were in Kendal, Mr. P. Wood, in front of your flap going through all the tricks of your trade.

FIRST MAN: It's you 'o's full of tricks. Well, it 'asn't come off. I'm not going to admit that.

SECOND MAN: You've admitted you weren't in Hull.

FIRST MAN: Yes.

SECOND MAN: Then if you weren't in Kendal, where were you?

FIRST MAN: What in May '60?

SECOND MAN: Yes.

FIRST MAN: Well, I

SECOND MAN: Come on, you must know.

FIRST MAN: I do know.

SECOND MAN: Out with it.

FIRST MAN: I was somewhere else.

SECOND MAN: That's a strange name for a town, where do you claim it is? In America?

FIRST MAN: No, no, it's just a matter of going back in me mind. I know where I was.

SECOND MAN: Out with it.

FIRST MAN: Brighouse.

SECOND MAN: A likely story.

FIRST MAN: Oh yes, I was.

SECOND MAN: Doing what?

FIRST MAN: Portering at the George.

SECOND MAN: Day or night?

FIRST MAN: Both.

SECOND MAN: You were never off duty?

FIRST MAN: I was sometimes. It was shift work. It was staggered.

SECOND MAN: That sounds dangerously unorthodox to me. Especially for Brighouse.

FIRST MAN: No, no, I did it out of choice. I asked them if I could do it that way. I was learning the ropes. I wanted to experience every facet of the game.

SECOND MAN: I know you're lying.

FIRST MAN: What's wrong with that? Why shouldn't porters get staggered?

SECOND MAN: It's not that.

FIRST MAN: Well, what?

SECOND MAN: It's the George. There's no hotel of that name in Brighouse.

FIRST MAN: Of course there is.

SECOND MAN: Don't tell me about Brighouse. I know it like the back of my hand, I can see it now, the esplanades, the old mausoleum, I can still smell the warm biscuity air wafting over from the flour mill. Please don't sully that town with

36

your deceits. Better men than you have passed through it, albeit rapidly. Come on, own up, you were never there.

FIRST MAN: I have been there.

SECOND MAN: But not in the month we're speaking of. Not at the non-existent George. Come on, I've caught you out. Nothing to be ashamed of. It was a good try. Anyone but my good self would have been fooled. But few men know their Brighouse as I do.

FIRST MAN: Well

SECOND MAN: You were elsewhere.

FIRST MAN: All right.

SECOND MAN: Where?

FIRST MAN: Hull.

SECOND MAN: Ah.

FIRST MAN: Yes, the story I told at first was true

SECOND MAN: In that case who was the man with the counterfeit false eye in Kendal and who was the man with the green biro in Hull?

FIRST MAN: Easy. The man in Hull was Manson. And the man with you was my brother, Dermot Galloway.

SECOND MAN: Under a different name.

FIRST MAN: Yes, 'e'd changed it.

SECOND MAN: Changed it to Wood. P. Wood.

FIRST MAN: Yes.

SECOND MAN: And what about Peddy?

FIRST MAN: Well, I changed my name to that.

SECOND MAN: Why?

FIRST MAN: The Chinese crowd.

SECOND MAN: And Ormeroyde?

FIRST MAN: He was the year before.

SECOND MAN: Where?

FIRST MAN: It was

SECOND MAN: Don't say Brighouse.

FIRST MAN: No, I

SECOND MAN: Leave that town alone.

FIRST MAN: Yes, yes. No, 'e was 'ere in this city. 'Ere in Leeds.

SECOND MAN: Is this Leeds?

FIRST MAN: Of course it is.

SECOND MAN: Excuse me whilst I note that down.

FIRST MAN: Ormeroyde 'ad nothing to do with what 'appened in Hull.

SECOND MAN: And what about this mysterious guest?

FIRST MAN: Oh, I made 'im up.

SECOND MAN: Weren't there any real guests at the Palm Court?

FIRST MAN: Of course there were.

SECOND MAN: Then why go to the trouble of inventing one?

FIRST MAN: Well

SECOND MAN: I don't mind telling you in my opinion such behaviour is tantamount to that of a novelist.

FIRST MAN: Oh no

SECOND MAN: Oh yes. I won't mince words.

FIRST MAN: No, no, I only used 'im as an excuse

SECOND MAN: Well, I suppose that mitigates it to some extent.

FIRST MAN: Of course it does. I only used 'im as an excuse t' make it seem as though I wasn't there. T'show 'ow I could know all about it without 'avin' been there.

SECOND MAN: And why did you wish to do that?

FIRST MAN: Because . . . Because I knew you weren't the real Manson. And if I'd behaved as if you were then I'd 'ave 'ad to take you in. And that would 'ave spoilt all me chances. All me chances when I come up against the real Manson. I wouldn't stand a chance with the police when I take the real Manson in if I'd already taken a Manson in before.

SECOND MAN: You've got a point there. The same would apply to me if I took you in instead of your brother.

FIRST MAN: That's it. We're both in the same boat.

SECOND MAN: So you and I have never actually met before today.

FIRST MAN: No, we only thought we 'ad.

SECOND MAN: I never thought we had.

FIRST MAN: Then why did you give me all that guff about me bein' in Kendal with the flap and the trout and all that?

SECOND MAN: I wanted to find out how much you knew of your brother's nefarious career.

FIRST MAN: Y' mean y' guessed I 'ad a brother?

SECOND MAN: Yes. I must say that until today, apart from the

38

few halcyon days I spent fishing with him, your brother's life has been a closed book to me.

FIRST MAN: Oh yeh, must 'ave been.

SECOND MAN: Strange in a way that you and he should be related. Because of course your own celebrated saga is an irradicable fixture of my mental furniture.

FIRST MAN: Eh?

SECOND MAN: Indeed I'd be lost without it.

FIRST MAN: What are y' talking about?

SECOND MAN: I'm saying that the mile-posts of your career are as the ABC to me.

FIRST MAN: But we've never met before. You've just said so.

SECOND MAN: Of course we've never met.

FIRST MAN: Then what are y' getting at?

SECOND MAN: But that doesn't mean I don't know who you are.

FIRST MAN: What d'you

SECOND MAN: My dear fellow you can't disguise your identity. Though it's very becoming that you should try. More than that it's endearing. One sees now why you're so popular. I recognized you long before you joined me at this table. Though of course I had no intention of making it known. One doesn't intrude upon the justly celebrated in their snatched and only too rare moments of privacy. It is sufficient honour to observe them unnoticed.

FIRST MAN: Now look 'ere

SECOND MAN: Dear fellow have no fear that I am going to crow it out at the top of my voice. After the signal honour you've done me in stooping to converse with me on the humdrum level which is the only one I'm capable of, it would be crass of me to broadcast your identity. But for my own private pleasure, as a special favour, please acknowledge—you can do it in the faintest whisper whilst no one else is looking—please confirm my conviction that you are indeed *he*.

FIRST MAN: Who?

SECOND MAN: Ah you play the game to the end. It's exactly what I would have expected of you. Everything I've read, the photographs, the signature—in photostat of course—

all give the same impression. Utterly steadfast in every thought, word, gesture, and deed. Now I know why Chamberlain made his famous remark.

FIRST MAN: What was that?

SECOND MAN: Haha. Such a question would be affectation in anyone else. But from you. Mmm. I shall savour it to the end of my days. I understand now the depth of your reticence. No need to actually say in so many words, that I am in the presence of—a wink will do it. When I ask you again, presumptuous though it is of me, when I ask you again will you be so good as to simply wink an eye? The left will do, don't waste the right on me. You are the gentleman I think you are?
Thank you. I thought so.

FIRST MAN: I didn't wink.

SECOND MAN: No more need be said, sir. I saw it. And I thank you for it.

FIRST MAN: Oh well.

SECOND MAN: From the bottom of my heart.

FIRST MAN: Oh . . . 's all right.

SECOND MAN: May I, I know it's a lot to ask but this is such a precious opportunity for me, may I intrude upon your good patience just a little further and ask you just one or two simple questions? Just to clear up a few points that have puzzled me and many others over the years. Probably because we're simple-minded rather than that there's any mystery, points that have bemused me on many an uneventful train journey.

FIRST MAN: Well, it depends.

SECOND MAN: You can couch your replies in veiled terms. A nod's as good as a wink to a whatever-it-is. And I shall treat all that you are good enough to divulge with the utmost secrecy.

FIRST MAN: Well

SECOND MAN: Please.

FIRST MAN: All right.

SECOND MAN: Thank you.

FIRST MAN: Oh, it's . . . nothing.

SECOND MAN: Well, here goes. When you went to the Palace the second time, is it true that you already knew about the Fluchenhauer Communiqué?

FIRST MAN: Er . . . yes, yes, I 'ad a fair idea.

SECOND MAN: Ah. May I dare to just press a little further. Please say if it's beyond the bounds of . . . but did you actually have a copy of it in your pocket? I mean that's often been suggested.

FIRST MAN: No, no, I didn't.

SECOND MAN: Amazing. That throws the machinations of the so called dissident faction into a completely new light.

FIRST MAN: Yes, well I suppose it does.

SECOND MAN: Tell me, what were your personal feelings at the time? What does it feel like to be in that sort of position? What goes on inside so to speak?

FIRST MAN: Well, it . . . it er makes you 'ungry.

SECOND MAN: Amazing. One imagines that all sort of complicated thoughts, emotions, policies, must crowd through the mind at such a critical moment. The man in the street imagines that key participants must be uplifted and sustained by a sense of History, of Destiny in the making. But in reality the dominant sensation is a desire for food.

FIRST MAN: Well, it was in my case.

SECOND MAN: And did you manage to get any during those critical hours?

FIRST MAN: Oh, I found the odd sandwich.

SECOND MAN: Where? If I may

FIRST MAN: In the palace. In the palace.

SECOND MAN: And now of course, these days, you lead a quieter life. I mean it would break the back of any normal man, but relatively speaking. Apart from TV and the syndicated column you take it easy?

FIRST MAN: Yeh. I try to.

SECOND MAN: You keep out of the limelight.

FIRST MAN: As far as I can.

SECOND MAN: Very wise. Do many people recognize you?

FIRST MAN: Oh, quite a few.

SECOND MAN: But you don't acknowledge it?

41

FIRST MAN: Only if they insist. If they pressure me I'll say one
    or two bits of things.
SECOND MAN: If they behave like I've just done in fact.
FIRST MAN: Well
SECOND MAN: I'm a swine.
FIRST MAN: Oh, no. I'm used to it.
SECOND MAN: Must be, must be. But you get no pleasure out of
    being the centre of attention?
FIRST MAN: Well, no, not nowadays. I used to when I first
    started off but it becomes second nature.
SECOND MAN: Yes, I can appreciate that. You select humble
    cafés like this on purpose?
FIRST MAN: In the main.
SECOND MAN: So that you won't be disturbed.
FIRST MAN: Yes.
SECOND MAN: Then what was it made you come over to me?
FIRST MAN: Well, I liked the look of you.
SECOND MAN: In what way?
FIRST MAN: Well, I thought you looked like a good sport.
SECOND MAN: A mutation?
FIRST MAN: No, no, a good sport, a good sort. A bloke 'o likes
    a good laugh.
SECOND MAN: So you came over for a laugh.
FIRST MAN: That's right. That's why I told you all the rubbish
    about Hull.
SECOND MAN: It was all a joke?
FIRST MAN: Yeh, that's it. It was all a leg pull.
SECOND MAN: Of course I should have guessed. You're famous
    for your practical jokes. It's dealt with in all the
    authenticated accounts.
FIRST MAN: Oh, aye, it will be.
SECOND MAN: Yes indeed. One last little indulgence. You've been
    so kind I hardly dare ask but it would set the seal on a
    wonderful experience. Will you please say, just once, very
    quietly, "I am" and then that celebrated name of yours?
FIRST MAN: Well, I
SECOND MAN: A compromise. Just say the surname.
FIRST MAN: No, you say the surname.

SECOND MAN: And then will you say the first name?

FIRST MAN: Uh . . . Look if you'll say the whole name first I'll say the whole name after.

SECOND MAN: I'd rather hear it from you first.

FIRST MAN: We'll both say the 'ole name together.

SECOND MAN: Ah it wouldn't be the same as hearing it from your own lips. I wouldn't be able to concentrate on listening if I was speaking at the same time.

FIRST MAN: All right say the name and I'll say it after.

SECOND MAN: Half each. That's fair.

FIRST MAN: No.

SECOND MAN: Oh, sir. It's been such a privilege meeting you and eavesdropping on the secrets of history. Don't tarnish my memory of it by denying me this little request.

FIRST MAN: Oh

SECOND MAN: You will?

FIRST MAN: I suppose so.

SECOND MAN: How generous.

FIRST MAN: Half each.

SECOND MAN: Very well. I'll say the first name. Sir Horace . . . Please don't keep me in suspense.

FIRST MAN: No . . . well . . . Bulstrode.

SECOND MAN: Oh, really!

FIRST MAN: What's the matter?

SECOND MAN: Really, sir. I kept my part of the bargain. I know you enjoy joking but at a serious and one might say even sacred moment like this I thought you'd do me the courtesy of replying in good faith.

FIRST MAN: I did.

SECOND MAN: Oh, come come, sir, you insult me. Anyone in this café could tell me your real name.

FIRST MAN: Ah no, they couldn't. Y'see the name you're thinking of that's not me real name. Bulstrode's the—that's the one I was born with. The other name's just for the public.

SECOND MAN: Oh, I see. So in fact you're doing me a special honour in giving me your secret and presumably family name.

FIRST MAN: Yes, yes, I thought y'd realize that.

43

SECOND MAN: Oh, well, I'm sorry, I apologize. It's just that Bulstrode's not mentioned in any of the standard biographies.

FIRST MAN: No, well, I kept it out of there.

SECOND MAN: May I ask why?

FIRST MAN: Well, y'see, one of my uncles was Admiral Bulstrode.

SECOND MAN: Was he?

FIRST MAN: Er . . . 'ave y' come across 'im?

SECOND MAN: I have indeed. Wasn't he on board the flagship at the Battle of Prague?

FIRST MAN: Yes, that was 'im.

SECOND MAN: Went down with it, too, if my memory serves me correctly.

FIRST MAN: Yes, very sad business for the family.

SECOND MAN: Must have been. Though of course he'd won the engagement before he went down.

FIRST MAN: Oh, aye.

SECOND MAN: Of course you're rather too young to remember it directly.

FIRST MAN: Oh, aye, but I've seen the newsreels of it.

SECOND MAN: Really. They must have been some of the first, 1813 wasn't it? The date of the engagement?

FIRST MAN: Was it? Well, I forget exactly. I meant paintin's, paintin's of it. Paintin's, newsreels, they're all more or less the same. Just ships and spray. Anyway we 'ad pictures of it all around the house. And of course I 'eard tell of it from an early age.

SECOND MAN: Must have been an essential part of the family lore.

FIRST MAN: Oh, yes, it was. And that's the very reason why I changed me name. Y'see I didn't want t'be confused with the other famous Bulstrode.

SECOND MAN: Didn't want to wither in the shadow of your illustrious ancestor.

FIRST MAN: That's exactly what it was.

SECOND MAN: So you adopted Frrrm as your public name?

FIRST MAN: Yes, I adopted Fern as me name. Sir Horace Fern.

SECOND MAN: I said Froom.

FIRST MAN: Well, we pronounce it Fern. It's one of those old-fashioned ways of pronouncing.

SECOND MAN: Oh, I see. But who are we?

FIRST MAN: Well, the family.

SECOND MAN: But Bulstrode's the family name.

FIRST MAN: Ah yes, but Fern comes down from me grandmother's side. That's where I got it from.

SECOND MAN: Sir Horace Fern.

FIRST MAN: Haha, y' managed to wheedle it out of me in the end.

SECOND MAN: Yes, yes, now I know exactly who you are.

FIRST MAN: Aye well.

SECOND MAN: But you still don't know who I am.

FIRST MAN: Y're Frank Thornton.

SECOND MAN: Afraid not.

FIRST MAN: Eh

SECOND MAN: Afraid not.

FIRST MAN: Oh, y're not going to start saying y're Manson again.

SECOND MAN: Don't be ridiculous. Of course I'm not.

FIRST MAN: Well, A'm glad to 'ear that.

SECOND MAN: No. I'm your brother Dermot Galloway.

FIRST MAN: Y'what!

SECOND MAN: I'm your long lost brother Dermot Galloway.

FIRST MAN: I 'aven't got a brother! That was before. I've admitted 'o I am. All that other was before.

SECOND MAN: But we both know you're not Sir Horace Fern.

FIRST MAN: Now look it was you 'o said I was in the first place.

SECOND MAN: I

FIRST MAN: All that about palaces, all that about what I'd done. Y' said y'd read about me. Seen me on

SECOND MAN: I'm afraid I got carried away. It was all wishful thinking. I'd always wanted to meet Sir Horace Fern. So much so that I allowed the impulse to carry me away. But I knew all along that you couldn't possibly be him.

FIRST MAN: Well, 'ow can y' be sure? I mean I must look pretty much like 'im.

SECOND MAN: In the first place he's dead. I attended the funeral.

45

It was the nearest I ever got to him. And in the second place I knew all along that you were my long lost twin brother Desmond Galloway.

FIRST MAN: Now look I've 'ad enough of this. Y' say y're one thing and then y'turn right round and say y're another.

SECOND MAN: But now the masquerade has ceased. And I sit before you as my real self.

FIRST MAN: Now listen.

SECOND MAN: How long ago it all seems. The running away. Bare feet over the cobbled street. Up to the orphanage. Flannel nightshirt and cod liver oil. I remember the last time I saw you. That last backward glance before I climbed for ever over the side of our mutual cot.

FIRST MAN: Y're mad. Y' must be. We're nothing like.

SECOND MAN: Ah, the vagaries of our differing paths have wrought their changes. Environment has lengthened a nose, chewed an ear, warped a limb. But I am happy in the knowledge that beneath these incidentals the matrix is the same.

FIRST MAN: I've never 'ad a brother!

SECOND MAN: I've returned.

FIRST MAN: Oh, I'm not

SECOND MAN: You want to go. Of course you want to move to somewhere more intimate. We can't really talk here. Where shall we go?

FIRST MAN: You're not coming with me!

SECOND MAN: Where shall we go? Oh, we've so much to tell each other. All those years to fill in. Oh, I can't wait. Come on let's be off. There's nothing to keep us here.

FIRST MAN: Ough!

SECOND MAN: Why are you sitting down again?

FIRST MAN: Now look, mister.

SECOND MAN: It's the excitement of reunion. You can't trust your legs yet. I know how it is.

FIRST MAN: Now look, mister—I'll come clean

SECOND MAN: All these years we've been separated. Oh, I can't tell you how I've longed for this moment. How I've lain awake

46

FIRST MAN: Listen. I never thought I knew you. When I came over at first and said I was Peddy

SECOND MAN: I've cried myself to sleep wondering where you were.

FIRST MAN: I never meant it. Any of it. It was all made up. I knew y' weren't a con man. I've never met one. It's just a game. A sort of thing A do. Just to get a bit of attention.

SECOND MAN: I'll stay with you tonight, tomorrow night, for ever.

FIRST MAN: I've done it before. It's just something in me 'ead. I 'alf convince meself but really A know. But every other time nothing's 'appened. They usually just ignore me or go away. A'm sorry, mister

SECOND MAN: Oh, dear brother, we shall never be parted again.

FIRST MAN: It's just that A'm a nonentity. That's why A do it. It was all made up. A'm sorry, mister. A'm sorry

SECOND MAN: I can hardly contain myself.

FIRST MAN: Listen! Listen! A'm tellin' you the truth!

SECOND MAN: We'll go and have a meal. Then we'll go to your place.

(*From here on they are both talking at the same time*)

FIRST MAN: I don't know you. I never did. Look, stop it. I'm not

SECOND MAN: I'll tell you about my days in the East . . . Oh

FIRST MAN: I 'aven't got a brother. Y'don't know me. Listen, I'm

SECOND MAN: we have so much to confide. But it's good to

FIRST MAN: tellin' you the bloody truth. Stop it. I've never 'ad

SECOND MAN: see you again. I want to take you by the

FIRST MAN: Listen will you. I've never seen y' before. I'm sorry

SECOND MAN: hand and make up for all these lost years.

(*Lights start to Fade Out.*)

FIRST MAN: I'm not. I'm not. Y'know A'm not. Listen t' me

SECOND MAN: Nothing can part us now. Absolutely nothing. I've

FIRST MAN: Please let me go. Please stop it. A'm sorry. Stop

SECOND MAN: been looking for you all these years. But

FIRST MAN: it. Stop it. I'm not. Please stop it

SECOND MAN: now I've found you. Yes, now I've found

BLACKOUT

A Discussion

CHARACTERS

Man
Woman

D

A Discussion was first performed by students from the Falmouth College of Art on the afternoon of 25th April 1969, at the Polytechnic Theatre, Falmouth.

MAN   David Westby
WOMAN   Elizabeth Oates

    Directed by David Halliwell
    Stage Manager Claire Williams

A Discussion was first performed by professionals at the Traverse Theatre, Edinburgh, on 14th May 1970, and was presented by the Traverse Theatre in Association with Quipu Productions Ltd.

MAN   Paul Freeman
WOMAN   Tina Packer

    Directed by Michael Rudman
    Stage Manager Gerry Jenkinson
    Set designed by Jean Ramsey

A bathroom. Bath, sink, lavatory, airing cupboard. Morning light through a glazed window. A man and a woman in their mid-thirties. He wears the bottom half of a pair of pyjamas and she wears the top half. Ideally this should be all, but underpants for him and bra for her are probably obligatory.

MAN: What y' talkin' about?
WOMAN: Y' know very well what A'm talkin' about.
MAN: A most certainly
WOMAN: Oh, yes, y' do.
MAN: A don't.
WOMAN: You know.
MAN: I 'av'n't the faintest
WOMAN: Oh, don't come
MAN: Now look
WOMAN: You look.
MAN: Me look.
WOMAN: Yes, you.
MAN: Why should A? You
WOMAN: Oh, aye, why should y'?
MAN: Yes. Why
WOMAN: Y' know very well.
MAN: A don't.
WOMAN: Y'do.
MAN: All right if I know
WOMAN: You know
MAN: Then what is it?
WOMAN: What's what?
MAN: What is it?

51

WOMAN: If y'know A don't need t'tell y'.

MAN: A don't know.

WOMAN: Y' said y' did.

MAN: When?

WOMAN: Just now.

MAN: A didn't.

WOMAN: Y' did.

MAN: A said nowt o' t' sort.

WOMAN: Then what did y' say?

MAN: When?

WOMAN: Just now.

MAN: A didn't say anything.

WOMAN: Y' did.

MAN: A didn't.

WOMAN: Y' did.

MAN: What did A say?

WOMAN: Y' said y' did.

MAN: Did what?

WOMAN: Did know.

MAN: A didn't.

WOMAN: Then what

MAN: A said

WOMAN: Don't

MAN: I said

WOMAN: Look don't

MAN: Let me finish.

WOMAN: 'O's stoppin' y'?

MAN: You are.

WOMAN: A'm not.

MAN: You are.

WOMAN: Go on, go on.

MAN: All right

WOMAN: Go ahead.

MAN: A will.

WOMAN: Do.

MAN: Right, A said A didn't.

WOMAN: What

MAN: I said I did not.

WOMAN: Don't talk like that.

MAN: Fuh . . . !

WOMAN: Didn't what?

MAN: Don't tell me . . . ! Y' know very well.

WOMAN: Very well what?

MAN: Y' know.

WOMAN: A don't.

MAN: Oh, so y' admit it.

WOMAN: Admit?

MAN: Yes, admit it.

WOMAN: Admit what?

MAN: Admit y' don't know.

WOMAN: A don't admit anything.

MAN: Oh, yes, y' did.

WOMAN: What?

MAN: That y' don't know what y're talkin' about.

WOMAN: Oh, no, A don't.

MAN: That's what A'm saying.

WOMAN: Sayin' what?

MAN: That y' don't know.

WOMAN: I know all right.

MAN: Y' just said y' didn't.

WOMAN: A know only too well.

MAN: Then why d' y' say y' didn't?

WOMAN: A didn't.

MAN: Y' did.

WOMAN: A said A didn't say A didn't A didn't say A didn't
    know.

MAN: Y' didn't say y' didn't say y' didn't!

WOMAN: A didn't say A didn't know.

MAN: Y' don't know what y' said.

WOMAN: Of course A do.

MAN: Then what was it?

WOMAN: Oh, yes, try t' switch it on t' me.

MAN: A'm not tryin'

WOMAN: As usual.

MAN: What a' y' talkin'

WOMAN: Your usual trick.

53

MAN: What trick?

WOMAN: Switch the blame.

MAN: It's no—you started it.

WOMAN: I started it?

MAN: Yes, you started by

WOMAN: 'Ow could I start it?

MAN: Y' said

WOMAN: A'm not talkin' about what I said

MAN: Well

WOMAN: A'm talkin' about what you did.

MAN: A don't know what

WOMAN: Oh, stop being so . . . coy.

MAN: Coy?

WOMAN: Yes, coy.

MAN: Coy! Y' think this's bein' coy?

WOMAN: Oh, stop

MAN: Y' don't know the meanin' of words.

WOMAN: A know what you're up to.

MAN: Up to?

WOMAN: Yes, cut it out.

MAN: A'm simply

WOMAN: We've 'ad it all before.

MAN: A'm just trying t' find out what y're talkin' about.

WOMAN: It doesn't work.

MAN: What a' y'

WOMAN: Y' know very well.

MAN: All right you tell me.

WOMAN: Tell y'!

MAN: Yes, you tell me.

WOMAN: Tell y' what?

MAN: What y' mean.

WOMAN: Oh

MAN: Y' can't.

WOMAN: Oh can't A?

MAN: No, y' can't.

WOMAN: Y' think A can't.

MAN: A do.

WOMAN: You're so

54

MAN: Go on tell me.

WOMAN: Why should A?

MAN: Y' can't.

WOMAN: A can.

MAN: Go on then.

WOMAN: All right.

MAN: Go on.

WOMAN: A will.

MAN: Fine.

WOMAN: A will don't worry.

MAN: Right, go on.

WOMAN: Don't worry.

MAN: A'm all ears.

WOMAN: All right. You refused.

MAN: Refused.

WOMAN: A knew y' wouldn't accept it.

MAN: That's crap.

WOMAN: Go on deny it.

MAN: A've no intention of

WOMAN: Y' can't.

MAN: There's nothing t' deny.

WOMAN: Are y' tryin' to mek out y' didn't refuse?

MAN: No, A'm not.

WOMAN: Wonders'll never cease.

MAN: A'm sayin' 'e never offered.

WOMAN: 'E?

MAN: Aye.

WOMAN: 'O?

MAN: Well, they then, they.

WOMAN: Y' said 'e.

MAN: What does it matter?

WOMAN: 'O d' y' mean?

MAN: Oh, A'm not goin' mention anybody in partic'lar. They.
    It doesn't matter.

WOMAN: Oh, yes, it does.

MAN: It doesn't.

WOMAN: It means you admit somebody did offer.

MAN: A said 'e didn't.

WOMAN: 'O?

MAN: Oh, y' know.

WOMAN: A don't.

MAN: Guess.

WOMAN: Lovely legs?

MAN: Ron.

WOMAN: Yes. Mr. Tripod 'imself.

MAN: Don't call 'im that.

WOMAN: Oh, no, y' don't like that.

MAN: Now don't start on that.

WOMAN: Oh, no, we mustn't start on that.

MAN: You always bring things back to that.

WOMAN: Well, that's a very important subj

MAN: We aren't discussin' that.

WOMAN: We mustn't even discuss it.

MAN: We were discussin'

WOMAN: Ron an' 'is

MAN: We weren't discussin' Ron in that connection. Now y'
know. . . . That's it. No more. T' only point about Ron
A'm prepared to discuss is whether or not 'e offered.

WOMAN: 'E

MAN: 'E never showed t' slightest indication of offerin'

WOMAN: Then why did y' single 'im out then?

MAN: A didn't single 'im out.

WOMAN: Then why d' y' bring 'im up?

MAN: Oh, I dunno . . . becos A knew you'd try t' mek out 'e
'ad.

WOMAN: Why should

MAN: It's always Ron this and Ron that.

WOMAN: A never said a word about 'im.

MAN: Just becos 'e flashes

WOMAN: A thought we weren't talkin' about

MAN: A'm not talkin' about that, A'm talkin' about t'way 'e
parades 'imself, 'is money—not 'at 'e 'as any—an' 'is so
called wit

WOMAN: Well, you just sat there.

MAN: A did not.

WOMAN: At least Ron kept things goin'.

MAN: Oh, aye, 'e kept t'coffee goin', comin' an' goin', coffee,
coffee, coffee, some of 'em Gaelic!

WOMAN: No.

MAN: One of 'em was.

WOMAN: Well, a few coffees, what's

MAN: Nine, 'e 'ad nine.

WOMAN: Some 'ost you are countin' t' coffees.

MAN: A minute ago y' were criticizin' me for payin'.

WOMAN: Not for a few coffees.

MAN: Oh, that's your idea of invitin' a few friends out for a
meal, is it?

WOMAN: No A

MAN: They pay for their own food but y' buy 'em a coffee
t'wash it down with.

WOMAN: Friends! Y' call that gang friends.

MAN: They are my friends.

WOMAN: So Ron's a friend now?

MAN: No, not Ron but

WOMAN: Then why invite 'im?

MAN: Oh, 'e was just a makeweight but the rest

WOMAN: Maxwell! Binnie an' Bennie! Jean whatser

MAN: Yes, they are.

WOMAN: A can never tell which is Binnie an' which is Bennie.

MAN: Y' know very well which is

WOMAN: All out for what they can grab, that's all.

MAN: Oh, 'ow is it then they were all clamourin' t'pay then?

WOMAN: They weren't.

MAN: Y' said they were.

WOMAN: A said some offered, some, an' you refused.

MAN: 'O offered?

WOMAN: What about Maxwell?

MAN: Maxwell's never paid 'is wack in 'is life.

WOMAN: 'E got out 'is wallet.

MAN: 'E didn't.

WOMAN: A saw 'im.

MAN: 'E moved 'is 'and inside 'is jacket that's all, momentarily,
just like this, a fleetin' movement, that's all 'e ever does.

WOMAN: Oh, no.

57

MAN: It wasn't in there above a second in fact it never really went in at all.

WOMAN: A've just seen what you did an' A never thought you'd taken out y'r wallet.

MAN: 'E's a lot cleverer at it than I am.

WOMAN: Any excuse.

MAN: 'E doesn't even 'ave a wallet in there.

WOMAN: 'Ow d'you know?

MAN: A know where 'e keeps 'is money, A've known 'im for years an' A've been all over with 'im, 'e keeps it in 'is back pocket with a button always buttoned up.

WOMAN: Then if 'e's so mean why lavish a meal on 'im?

MAN: Well

WOMAN: If they're all so tight why

MAN: A didn't say they were all

WOMAN: If none of 'em offered.

MAN: A didn't say none of 'em offered.

WOMAN: Oh, yes, y' did.

MAN: Now look it was you.

WOMAN: It wasn't.

MAN: Y' never stick t'

WOMAN: It's you 'o doesn't stick.

MAN: 'Ow d' y' mek that out?

WOMAN: Y' know very well.

MAN: A don't know what y're talkin' about.

WOMAN: Oh, yes, y' do.

MAN: A don't.

WOMAN: 'Course y' do.

MAN: A don't.

WOMAN: Y' do.

MAN: What a' y'

BLACKOUT

Muck from Three Angles

CHARACTERS

Linda Carter
Margaret Kaye
James Gill

Muck from Three Angles was first performed at the Traverse Theatre, Edinburgh, on 14th May 1970, and was presented by the Traverse Theatre in association with Quipu Productions Ltd.

LINDA CARTER   Sheila Ballantine
MARGARET KAYE   Tina Packer
JAMES GILL   Jack Shepherd

    Directed by Michael Wearing
    Stage Manager Gerry Jenkinson
    Set designed by Jean Ramsey

Muck from Three Angles opened in London four days later on 18th May 1970, at the Quipu Basement Theatre, presented by Quipu Basement Theatre.

LINDA CARTER   Jan Edwards
MARGARET KAYE   Alex Marshall
JAMES GILL   Walter Hall

    Directed by David Calderisi
    Stage Manager Jay Browne

BLACKOUT. LINDA CARTER'S *voice is heard. It is taped.*

A remember it. That afternoon. 'Course A do. Very clear.
A've a very clear mem'ry of it. Yes, very clear. Oh, aye.
A c'n remember it.

SCENE ONE

LIGHTS UP ON: *A door frame containing a door. One side of the door frame is the street; the other side is a living-room. The living-room is represented by the following bright new rather garish furniture; two easy chairs, one upright chair, one table.* LINDA CARTER *sits in one of the easy chairs. She is about thirty, has short well-groomed blonde hair, is extremely clean-looking and is neatly and immaculately dressed in blouse, skirt and pinny. Her manner is pleasant, lively and relaxed.* MARGARET KAYE, *also about thirty, slumps lazily in the other chair. She has unkempt brown hair and is carelessly dressed in a shapeless sweater and a pair of worn trousers. She has an amiable but bovine expression on her face.*

LINDA: We've talked about sev'ral places. But we've still plenty
    time t'mek up us minds. A don't know, A'm not fussy. As
    long as it's sunny an' peaceful it'll do me. We might go
    abroad again this year.
MARGARET: But it's a right long way in't it, Linda?
LINDA: Where?
MARGARET: Abroad.

LINDA: Depends where y'go. We 'ave mentioned Spain.
   Apparently the's sum very nice beaches near Barcelona.
MARGARET: Well, A mean 'ow wud y' like manage t'get there,
   Linda?
LINDA: We cud fly A suppose.
MARGARET: Oo A wun't want t' like go up in an airoplane.
LINDA: Oh, it's very pleasant. Y'don't
   (*The doorbell chimes.*)
MARGARET: That's sumdy at y' door, Linda.
LINDA: A wunder 'o it c'n be?
   (*She opens the door.* JAMES GILL *stands outside. He is about
   thirty-five, medium height, has flat hair. He is dressed in a
   dirty light brown old-fashioned belted raincoat, dirty old-
   fashioned wide flannel trousers with turn-ups, a scarf wound
   tightly round his neck, a flat cloth cap on his head, and a
   pair of dark tinted spectacles.*)
   (*He is standing perfectly still, his head thrust forward
   aggressively from slightly hunched shoulders. His face has a
   lean quality, a tautness about the cheeks. He has a tightly set
   thin-lipped mouth and his eyes gimlet from behind his
   spectacles. He carries a small battered suitcase under one
   arm.*)
GILL: God sent me.
LINDA: A beg y' pardon?
GILL: A'm sellin' on beyarf o' t' Lord.
LINDA: Oh, A see.
   (*He pushes past her and strides into the room.*)
GILL: It's God's work. All t' proceeds go t' charity.
   (*He places the case on the table.* LINDA *closes the door.*)
LINDA: T' charity.
GILL: Aye. 'Elp others. It's God's will. Buy.
LINDA: Well. That depends. Wot 'ave y' got?
   (*He snaps the case open.*)
GILL: Stuff y' need.
MARGARET: Oo it sounds right int'restin'.
   (*He snatches an old dirty frayed newspaper from the case
   and thrusts it at* LINDA.)
GILL: This.

LINDA: Wot is it?

GILL: Are y' blind? *Briggus Echo.*

LINDA: But it's all torn.

GILL: Buy it.

LINDA: Feb'ry 20th, 1964. It's sev'ral years old.

GILL: Cut t' cackle. Mek an offer.

LINDA: An offer?

MARGARET: Wot sort of an offer d' y' mean like?

GILL: 'S foh God. Cum on.

LINDA: Well, A'm sorry. But A don't really think

GILL: Think. 'O d' y' think y'are? Don't fuck me about.

LINDA: Now really

GILL: All right. As a special concession, Mrs. Faddy.

(*He drops the paper back into the case and pulls out an old 78 gramophone record with a hefty chip out of the edge.*)
Music.

LINDA: But it's cracked.

GILL: Blackbottom Stomp. Cum on.

MARGARET: Ee it duz look an odd shape.

LINDA: It's got a g't big chip out of it.

GILL: Duzn't matter. Y' c'n still play two-thirds. Buy it.

LINDA: No. Why shud A?

(*He moves towards her.*)

GILL: Don't quibble. Buy.

(*She retreats.*)

LINDA: No. A won't. Please go.

GILL: Don't waste God's time. Buy.

(*He advances.*)

LINDA: No. Get away.

GILL: Y'd better.

LINDA: Get away.

GILL: Cum on. Give.

(LINDA *suddenly stops and stands her ground.* GILL *stops.*)

LINDA: Y're not sellin' foh charity. Y're just on t' make. Ow dare y' cum in t' my 'ouse.

GILL: Wot?

LINDA: 'Ow dare y'. Cum on. Get out.

GILL: God dun't like this.

LINDA: God dun't know owt about it. If y're not out o' this 'ouse in fifteen seconds A'll call t' police.

GILL: All right. But God'll not forget. Don't think 'E will. Y've insulted 'Is salesman.

(*He puts the record back in the case and closes the lid.*)

LINDA: Salesman!

MARGARET: Wait a minute, Linda, A'd like t'know wot 'e means like by sayin' 'e's God's salesman like.

LINDA: Oh, don't be daft, Marg'ret.

GILL: It's a good question. It's not 'er 'o's daft.

LINDA: 'E's lyin', Marg'ret.

GILL: That's blasphemous.

MARGARET: But A mean 'ow can y' know like?

GILL: She dun't. She's blind.

LINDA: A'm not. 'E's a fake.

GILL: God appointed me 'Imself. A c'n tell y' 'ow it 'appened.

MARGARET: Can y'?

LINDA: Don't listen to 'im. Cum on move.

GILL: She wants t'.

MARGARET: Aye A'd like t' 'ear 'ow it 'appened like.

LINDA: Marg'ret Kaye be y'r age.

MARGARET: A'd just like t' 'ear it like.

GILL: Y're shrewd.

LINDA: Oh, okay. But mek it snappy.

(*She sits down and watches* GILL *with amused sarcasm.* MARGARET *listens enthralled to the following; reacting with noises of appreciative awe whenever called for.*)

GILL: God sent me a sign. It were three years ago. One 'ot, dark, oppressive night. A woh lyin' on me bed. A cudn't sleep. Sweat woh pourin' out of me. A lay there flat on me back, starin' into the blackness. The' was no light, no sound, no movement. Ev'ry thing was still, dark, silent an' eery. As A lay there a conception came t' me. A decided t' challenge t'Deeity. A decided t' test God. A called upon 'Im t' reveal 'Is existence by sending me a sign. A sed out loud, "God, if y' exist, send an 'and t' grasp me foot" . . . A 'eld me breath. A waited. I imagined an enormous fist surrounded by flames might cum crashin' through t' wall

64

wi' a shatterin' thunder. But seconds ticked by, tick, tick, tick. Then minutes. Nothing 'appened. A fell asleep w'out knowin' it. Suddenly I awoke. At first A didn't realize why. But then A became aware—there was an 'and wrapped round my foot. Aye. A 'uman 'and. My own! My own 'and was grasped round my own foot. God never duz t' obvious. 'E'd sent me a sign in 'Is own way.

MARGARET: Eee A think that's, ooh, A think it's marv'llous A

LINDA: A real miracle, eh?

GILL: Aye.

MARGARET: Aye, that's right, Linda, a miracle that's wot it musta been.

LINDA: A miracle my foot. Never mind 'is. It woh no miracle.

MARGARET: But, Linda

LINDA: If it 'appened at all y' just did it t' y'self.

GILL: No. Why shud A?

LINDA: Mebbe becos y' think y' are God.

GILL: Blasphemy.

MARGARET: Y' don't think that do y'?

GILL: No.

LINDA: A think it's just a tale.

GILL: No!

MARGARET: But why shud 'e like

LINDA: So them 'at's green be'ind t' lug oyls such as you'll gobble it up an' buy t' muck 'e's pinched from folks' dustbins.

GILL: That's libel

MARGARET: Oo 'e'd 'ave t' be very clever t'make sumthing like all that up.

LINDA: It's amazin' wot sum minds a' capable of.

GILL: Don't listen to 'er. It 'appened.

MARGARET: It sounds very convincin'.

LINDA: Marg'ret.

GILL: God instructed me t'sell for 'Im.

MARGARET: Foh charities like?

GILL: Aye.

LINDA: 'E pockets t'money 'is sen

GILL: A don't.

MARGARET: A shudn't think 'at 'e duz like Linda.

LINDA: Don't be so soft.

> (GILL *snatches from the case a cardboard tube from the*
> *centre of a toilet roll and flourishes it at* MARGARET.)

GILL: Buy foh God.

LINDA: T' cardboard tube from t' middle of a toilet roll!

GILL: Buy foh t' Lord.

MARGARET: Awright then A'll 'ave it.

GILL: Fifteen bob.

LINDA: Oh, no, y' don't.

> (*She snatches the tube from him.*)

GILL: Ey!

MARGARET: Wot.

LINDA: A'm not lettin' y' line 'is pockets. 'E 'as nowt t'do wi'
God.

GILL: Libel. Blasphemy. Y' can't prove it.

LINDA: Oh can't A?

GILL: Y' can't.

LINDA: Oh well, we'll see about that.

MARGARET: Wot d' y' mean, Linda?

GILL: 'S just bluff.

LINDA: We'll see. A'm goin' t' conduct a little test. We'll see
'o's tellin' t' truth.

MARGARET: But 'ow, Linda?

GILL: Bluff.

> (*She raises the tube above her head.*)

LINDA: A'm goin' t'ask God t' strike me paralysed if this bloke
really is 'Is salesman.

GILL: No. No. Y' mun't. It cud be fatal.

MARGARET: Oo, Linda, A shudn't.

LINDA: If A'm struck 'e's tellin' t' truth. If A'm not I'm tellin'
it.

GILL: God may not be in t' mood.

LINDA: Oh, aye, 'E will. If you're as important as y' say y' are
an' 'E really is be'ind y'. A mean god'd 'ardly leave y' in t'
lurch, wud 'E?

> (GILL *has no reply.*)

MARGARET: Oo, Linda.

66

LINDA: Shh. God, I challenge you; if this man is really your salesman give us a sign by striking me rigid wi' paralysis in t' next five minutes.

(*She smiles with confidence at them. Cheerfully certain that nothing is going to happen.* MARGARET *is awestruck.* GILL *watches uneasily. Seconds go by.* LINDA'*s smile broadens, after about twenty seconds* MARGARET *starts to relax a fraction. Then suddenly* LINDA *jerks as if struck by an invisible force, has a rapid spasm, tries fleetingly to move and freezes into rigidity.* GILL *and* MARGARET *let out noises of alarm and astonishment. Utterly horrified. They stare. Then suddenly* LINDA *breaks into laughter.*)

MARGARET: Ooo, Linda, ooo.

GILL: A trick!

LINDA: Aye, y' dozy beggers.

MARGARET: Oo y'did give me a turn.

LINDA: Y'deserve it foh bein' so gullible.

GILL: Well

MARGARET: A suppose like it was really funny really.

LINDA: Aye. Oo. A feel a strange compulsion in me 'ands. A can't stop 'em.

(*She picks up* GILL'*s case and carries it to the door.*)

GILL: Ey! Stop! That's mine! Wot a'y' doin'?

(LINDA *opens the door*).

LINDA: Oo A just can't 'elp it. Summat's directin' me 'ands. A can't control 'em.

(MARGARET *is amused.*)

A can't control 'em.

(*She hurls the suitcase through the door.*)

GILL: No!

LINDA: Ee wot a pity. But the's no stoppin' these mysterious forces once they got goin'.

GILL: Y've no right!

(*He rushes out after the case.*)

LINDA: It woh nowt t'do wi' me. Good afternoon. Call again when y've got some new lines.

(*She slams the door. Turns to* MARGARET *who is giggling.*)

Eee, Margaret.

(*They laugh together.* BLACKOUT.)

(*We hear* GILL's *voice, on tape.*)
I remember a call A made one afternoon. It was to an 'ouse in one o' the streets in this vicinity. I can remember this particular 'ouse. It was in the afternoon when I arrived there.

SCENE TWO

LIGHTS UP ON: *The street side of the door. The room is in darkness.* GILL *stands serenely before the door. He holds himself up with dignity. His neck is not shrunk into his shoulders, his shoulders are not hunched, he does not stoop. The expression on his face is bland and benign. He wears ordinary spectacles which are neither old-fashioned, thick-lensed, nor darkly tinted. He carries his suitcase by the handle.* GILL *knocks on the door. After a moment it opens.* LINDA *confronts him. She has a hard, mean, thin-lipped expression. Her hair is combed back severely. She glowers malevolently at* GILL. *He smiles at her and takes off his cap.*

LINDA: Wot y' want?
GILL: I'm workin' on beyarf of the Lord.
LINDA: Wot?
GILL: I'm selling things for charity.
LINDA: Clear off.
GILL: All proceeds go to the needy.
LINDA: I don't care. Shuv.
GILL: But surely, madam, you can spare sumthing for those less fortunate.
LINDA: No. A don't believe in charity. Get goin'. March. We don't want undesirables round 'ere.
(MARGARET *appears at the door. The light goes up on the living-room. Her hair is rather more attractively arranged and her clothes are somewhat better groomed than in Scene One. There is an indolent sexuality about her.*)
MARGARET: Why don't y' let the man cum in for a while, Linda?
LINDA: A'm not 'avin' 'im in.

68

MARGARET: 'E might 'ave one or two things t'show us.

GILL: My stock is simple.

MARGARET: Oh, let 'im show us wot 'e's got, it can't do any 'arm.

GILL: It won't take long.

LINDA: Oh.

MARGARET: Yes. Cum in.

(*He enters.*)

LINDA: A don't like it. Mek it snappy. An' don't touch owt.

(*He places his suitcase on the table.* MARGARET *has followed him to the table.* LINDA *shuts the door.*)

MARGARET: Y' goin' t'display all y'r goodies?

GILL: I'll show you wot I've got.

(*He takes out the old newspaper.*)

LINDA: Wot's that?

GILL: *Brig'ouse Echo.* Feb'ry twentieth 1964.

MARGARET: Wot's so special about that?

LINDA: It's rubbish.

GILL: It's not it's intrinsic value 'at counts.

LINDA: A don't even buy t'*Echo* new.

GILL: It's the spiritual value. As a token of charity given an' received.

MARGARET: Spiritual value?

LINDA: Givin's stupid. A wun't give anybody anythin'.

GILL: P'raps something else might prove more suitable.

(*He puts the paper back in the case and takes out the 78 gramophone record.*)

A little music?

LINDA: Music. A've no time foh music.

MARGARET: Wot's it called?

GILL: Blackbottom Stomp. Jelly Roll Morton an' 'is Red 'ot Peppers.

LINDA: Muck.

MARGARET: That sounds like sumthing A cud use.

GILL: The line up's good; George Mitchell cornet, Johnny Dodds clarinet, Kid Ory trombone

MARGARET: God approves duz 'E?

GILL: God duz.

LINDA: God. The's no such thing.

GILL: Wot makes you so sure?

LINDA: It's too daft t' credit. It's just put about by undesirables.

GILL: Undesirables?

LINDA: Things like you. Why don't y' get back where y' cum from?

GILL: But A cum from Brig'ouse just like you.

LINDA: Y' lyin' sod.

GILL: No, it's the truth. I was born down Mill Lane.

LINDA: Y' cheeky beggar. Get out o' my 'ouse. Get back t' y' foul den an' carr down wi' all t'other niggers.

GILL: Y' can't rile me by comparin' me to our dark-skinned brothers.

LINDA: Brothers. Animals more like.

GILL: May God ease your pain.

LINDA: Pain. T' ony pain A've got 's pain in me eyes at sight o' your ugly dial. Get out o' my 'ouse y' yid, nigger, buggerist or whatever y'are.

GILL: On the Lord's beyarf an' on my own I forgive you, sister.

LINDA: Gerrout.

MARGARET: No, wait a minute, Linda, you go an' get on with y' work. A'd just like to see wot else 'e's got. A'll keep me eye on him.

LINDA: Well

MARGARET: A won't let him stay long.

LINDA: Well, don't. A'll go an' polish t' stove. Mek sure y're not 'ere when A get back, Sambo.

(*She exits.*)

MARGARET: Sit y'self down.

GILL: A thought y' wanted t' see sum further items.

MARGARET: A do but the's no rush.

GILL: For a minute then, thank you.

(*He sits on the upright chair.*)

MARGARET: My name's Margaret.

GILL: A fine old name.

MARGARET: Wot's yours?

GILL: Gill.

MARGARET: First name?

GILL: James.

70

MARGARET: Tell me more about y'self, James.

GILL: I'm dedicated t'doing the Lord's work.

MARGARET: Y' mean sellin' things like this?

GILL: Yes. The Lord appointed me to do it.

MARGARET: 'Ow did that 'appen?

GILL: 'E sent me a sign.

MARGARET: In a dream?

GILL: No. One night. A cudn't sleep. So

MARGARET: Were y' sleepin' on y'r own?

GILL: Of course.

MARGARET: All sorts of strange things 'appen t'people 'o sleep on their own. It's not altogether healthy.

GILL: I've never 'ad any problems.

MARGARET: None at all?

GILL: No. But to return to the night in question. I asked God if 'E'd send me a sign of 'Is existence. I requested 'Im to send a hand to take 'old of my foot.

MARGARET: Your foot?

GILL: Yes. I fell asleep but when I awoke I found 'at I was 'oldin' my foot in my own hand.

MARGARET: Y're sure it was y'r foot y' were 'oldin'?

GILL: Certain. Not long afterwards 'E revealed to me why 'E'd given me a sign. 'E revealed 'Is desire that I shud renounce worldly pleasures an' dedicate myself t' raisin' money for the needy.

(MARGARET *gets up and walks over to him.*)

MARGARET: But surely not all worldly pleasures?

GILL: I'm afraid so.

(*He gets up.*)

MARGARET: But a big boy like you must 'ave inclinations.

GILL: My work consumes 'em.

MARGARET: All of 'em?

GILL: Er—yes.

MARGARET: Y' don't sound completely sure.

GILL: I am. I've renounced the flesh.

MARGARET: Don't y' like me?

GILL: You're . . . pleasant.

MARGARET: Is that all?

GILL: Well . . . you're

MARGARET: Y're a fine, big, strong lad. A woman cud really give 'erself wi' a man like you.

GILL: No. I

MARGARET: Why don't you 'elp me?

GILL: I can't.

MARGARET: God wants y' t'elp the needy an' I'm needy.

GILL: I . . . I can't.

MARGARET: Give me what A need.

GILL: I

MARGARET: A need y'

GILL: I

MARGARET: A need it

GILL: Ah

MARGARET: Please.

(GILL *is under great strain. He seems to be on the verge of taking hold of her. Then:*)

GILL: No!

MARGARET: Please, please, please

GILL: I'm sorry. Truly sorry. But I can't. I mustn't deviate from God's demands.

MARGARET: Ugh! Y' mek me sick! Y' dirty little toad!

GILL: May God bless you, Marg'ret.

MARGARET: Y' reckon y're so pure. Renounced the flesh! I think y' just 'av'n't got any balls!

GILL: Poor Marg'ret, I'm sorry I've 'ad t' hurt y'.

(LINDA *returns.*)

LINDA: A told you A didn't want t'see y' when A cum back.

MARGARET: Y' mek me puke.

GILL: Bless you.

LINDA: Wot's 'e been up to?

MARGARET: 'E insulted me.

GILL: Bless you.

LINDA: Y' shud be put down. Things like you. Y're not fit t' mix wi' decent folk. Y' mucky, shiftless bugger. Y're neither use t' y're sen nor t' nubbdy else. Y're an eyesore. Talk about God. If the' was such a thing 'E'd be on my side not yours. 'E'd back up decent folk not dirty niggers.

72

GILL: I shall pray for you.
   (*He closes his case.*)
MARGARET: Pray. Y've nowt between y' legs. Y' greasy little runt.
GILL: May the Lord smile on you.
LINDA: Get out. Y'mucky Nigger. A'd rather burn
   all me money 'an give it t' you. Y' cheap skate.
   Liar. Get out. Y' 'orrible little sod. Get out. Y'
   shud be shot. Shot. Shot.   *Speaking*
MARGARET: Y've no balls. Nowt but wind. A wudn't   *together*
   touch y'. 'Ow dare y' speak to a woman. Y've
   nowt to offer. Y're a toad. A toad. Ugly toad.
   Toad.
   (*As they scream at him,* GILL *with great serenity walks to
   the door, opens it, turns towards them and raises his arms in
   benediction.*)
GILL: May the Lord bless, keep, an' be with you for ever.
   (BLACKOUT.)

(*We hear* MARGARET's *voice, on tape.*)
A certainly remember the er afternoon that is er in
question. Oh, yes, A most certainly do recall it. If my
memory serves me correctly, and A think A'm right in er
thinkin' that it duz, then

SCENE THREE

LIGHTS UP ON: *The living-room.* MARGARET, *her hair and clothes
fairly tidy, sits calmly, comfortably but with dignity in one of the
easy chairs.* LINDA, *her hair and clothes slightly ruffled, sits nervous-
ly on the edge of the upright chair.*

MARGARET: I always say it's very nice t'be able t' put y'r feet up
   for a while in the afternoon.
LINDA: Aye. Well. So long as the's nowt needs
MARGARET: Oh relax, Linda.
LINDA: I am. I am.
MARGARET: You know wot they say—all work an' no play
   makes Jill into a dull erm girl.

73

LINDA: Aye. Shall A mek a cuppa?

MARGARET: No, no, Linda, you sit still, you sit in one of the er easy chairs an' A'll make the er tea.

LINDA: A'm all right sittin' 'ere. I am.

MARGARET: Relaxation is really the er secret of the full an' the 'appy er life.

LINDA: A suppose so.

(The doorbell chimes. LINDA *jumps up.)*

A wunder 'o that is?

(She rapidly glances round the room to make sure it's tidy, pats a cushion on the empty easy chair.)

Oh dear. If A'd know anybody were

(Hurries to the door. MARGARET *smiles.* LINDA *opens the door.* GILL *stands outside. He stands stiffly and perfectly still. His head is sunk into hunched, stooped, rounded shoulders. He appears to have no neck. His face seems heavy, flabby and stolid. He peers myopically through thick-lensed, old-fashioned spectacles. His raincoat looks shabbier and more shapeless than in other scenes. The belt has been removed and the pockets bulge, filled with rubbish. His cap seems rammed down tightly over his scalp. He carries his suitcase under his arm.)*

*(*LINDA *is alarmed at the sight of him. There is a pause during which neither of them speaks or moves.)*

GILL: A'm 'ere like. On beyarf. Like. Beyarf o't'. Like Deeity like.

LINDA: Eh?

GILL: A mean like. Sellin'. God's beyarf like. T' t'needy.

LINDA: Well

MARGARET: Is this for erm a charity?

(She gets up.)

LINDA: A don't

*(*MARGARET *arrives at the door.)*

GILL: Charity. Y'cud. Aye.

MARGARET: An' wot is it that you are sellin'?

GILL: Me case. In 'ere. Stuff like.

LINDA: Well, A'm sorry. But we're not

MARGARET: Oh, A don't know er, Linda, p'raps we might just 'ave a er look.

74

LINDA: No. No. A don't want

MARGARET: Just for a moment.

> (*She indicates to* GILL *that he may enter. He suddenly darts clumsily into the room.*)

LINDA: Marg'ret y'shudn't. A don't want t'

> (*stumbles but manages not to fall. However, in maintaining himself upright he plonks his case on the table.*)
>
> Be careful. Be careful wi' that table.

GILL: A'm sorry like.

MARGARET: It's really quite all right, Linda, y'know. A mean our er friend 'ere 'asn't dun any damage at all.

LINDA: 'S not your table. A don't want 'im in 'ere. A don't.

MARGARET: Well, A shudn't imagine that 'is er bizness shud really take all that er long really. May it be possible for us t'see now wot exactly it er is that you 'ave in your case there?

GILL: Aye.

LINDA: A don't want t'know.

> (GILL *fumbles with the catches of the case but can't get them open.*)

GILL: Dun't seem t' . . . Can't gerrit . . . Dun't cum like . . . T'rain 'as been 'eavy t'last . . . 'Ave t'rench like. Might be . . . Clive Robert's muther once 'ad t'open a case wi' a shoe 'orn.

MARGARET: Really. A must say your case duz seem rather stiff.

LINDA: Is the' any need t'open it?

> (GILL *starts to shake the case about.*)

GILL: Wunder. Can't . . . Summow . . . Mebbe it's t' temp'rature.

LINDA: Stop wavin' it about. The's dust cummin' off it.

MARGARET: Are y'sure you 'av'n't locked it maybe?

GILL: Aye. A've no key. Never 'ad.

LINDA: Stop it. Be careful. Mind t'table.

> (*Suddenly the case flies open. Bits of old wrapping paper, a couple of empty cigarette boxes, old frayed newspapers, a paperback minus its paper back, the cardboard tube from the centre of a toilet roll, an old worn toothbrush, all scatter round the table.*)

Oh. All over me carpet.

MARGARET: Oh, dear, but never mind.

GILL: A'll 'ave t'

(*He starts hurriedly and clumsily to pick things up.*)

LINDA: Oh, cum on. Cum on. Be quick. Get it all up.

GILL: Mun't leave nowt like. Shudda seen. But not till now. Like din't know.

(MARGARET *hands him a piece of paper.*)

MARGARET: 'Ere's one of your er things.

GILL: Ta. Can't see nowt else.

LINDA: A' these t' things y're tryin' t' sell?

GILL: Me stock.

LINDA: Stock. Y' call it stock.

MARGARET: Well, wud y'like p'raps now to er indicate one or two of your er items now, please?

(*He pulls out the old newspaper.*)

GILL: T'*Echo.*

LINDA: *Briggus Echo*?

GILL: Feb'ry t' twentieth 1963.

LINDA: A mucky old *Echo*. Years old.

GILL: Cud 'ave int'rest. Sum. Cud be.

LINDA: A can't believe it. A can't. It's unbelievable. 'Ow much a' y' askin' foh that?

GILL: Well. Mek me an offer, like.

LINDA: An offer. An offer. Mek y' an. Y'must think A'm barmy.

MARGARET: Now, Linda.

(GILL *replaces the paper in the case and takes out the old 78 with the chip out of the edge.*)

GILL: Mebbe y'd. Music.

LINDA: Music.

GILL: Blackbottom Stomp.

LINDA: Black wot? 'Ow dare y'. 'Ow dare y'.

MARGARET: It's only a title, really, Linda.

GILL: 'S Jam Roll Mortey's Red 'ot Pokers.

LINDA: 'Ow dare y'. In me own 'ouse.

GILL: George Marshall clarinet, Johnny Dobbs

LINDA: A can't believe me ears. A mucky cracked old record.

76

All these mucky names. A can't believe, A-A can't, A c-c-can't, c-c-can't

MARGARET: Linda, Linda, there's no need

(GILL *puts the record back into the case. He pulls out the cardboard tube from the centre of a toilet roll and proffers it to* LINDA. *She shrieks and goes into hysterics.*)

LINDA: Aah. No. N-no. Get out. Owowout. Oh. Oh. A c-c-c-can't, c-c-can't Owowow. Aaah.

(MARGARET *takes hold of* LINDA *by the arm and leads her to a chair into which she collapses weeping.* GILL *stands stiffly watching.*)

MARGARET: Y'll be all right now in a minute, Linda, just take it easy.

(*She turns to* GILL.)

Now er, Mister, er?

GILL: Er

MARGARET: Mister?

GILL: Like Gill.

MARGARET: Well, Mr. Gill, where are you er from then?

GILL: That street 'at runs parallel wi' East Street.

MARGARET: Oh, really. A see. But wot

GILL: By t'corner shop. Mrs. Ellis 'ad it. Sells sweets and all such stuff as that like. Novelties. A think they 'ad sum fireworks there at one time.

MARGARET: That's int'restin' but wot A really meant

GILL: Billy 'Inchcliffe woh tellin' me 'e even bought a disc there once. T'Parker Quintet wi' Dizzy on Esquire. It might 'a' been Miles but A think 'e said Diz. A don't know t'titles.

MARGARET: Wot a pity but wot A meant really, Mr. er Gill, was 'o was it that 'er sent you 'ere?

GILL: Well. As A sez. God. As A sez like.

MARGARET: So y'don't as it were represent sum kind of organization?

GILL: No. Just t'Deeity. Sellin' for 'Im.

MARGARET: And do the er proceeds go t'charities?

GILL: Aye.

MARGARET: Can you for instance tell me wot charities?

GILL: Well. Er. A gave eight bob t' t' Ebenezer. An' eleven bob for a gravestone foh Twinkles.

MARGARET: A'm sorry, for 'o?

GILL: Mrs. Rawcliffe's cat.

MARGARET: Well, that was very nice, Mr. Gill, but er tell me if y'don't really mind 'ow did you er arrive at the er comprehension that the er Lord wished you to go round sellin' things on His behalf?

GILL: A sign. Sumtime back. Three year ago. T'ottest since 1946. So they sed. That night like. A don't know if it woh but that's wot t'paper sed.

MARGARET: Three years ago on a warm night

GILL: Aye. T'ottest since 1946. So they sed like. A don't know if it woh but

MARGARET: Yes. And this was the night when

GILL: A'd been over t'Elland

MARGARET: Oh.

GILL: T'a session at t'Weavers. T'Weavers Arms. A think it were t'Weavers. The' woh Dave Sykes on banjo an' Bob Ainley on clarinet an'

MARGARET: A see. Was it.

GILL: The' woh a kid there brought some bongos but A di'n't know 'im.

MARGARET: No, but was it er in Elland you received this um sign?

GILL: No. That wor at 'ome. In me bedroom. This 'and came like. Well, it didn't cum. It woh me own. But it'd been directed. It grabbed me foot like. A cun't sleep. A'd been t'Elland t'evenin' before like. A went wi' Pete Mellor in 'is minivan. Red. It's painted red. Wi' cream mudguards. It 'asn't got any winders in t' sides.

MARGARET: 'Asn't it, A see. But after y'd returned

GILL: It 'as winders in t' front. In t' part where t' driver sits. An' sum int' back door.

MARGARET: Yes, but

GILL: But the's nowt in t' sides o' t' van part.

MARGARET: Yes, Mr. Gill, A do see what y' mean

GILL: Aye. A'd to ride in t' van part. Pete 'ad 'is trumpet-case up in front in t' seat beside 'im.

MARGARET: But when you finally returned t' your 'ome.

GILL: When we got t'Elland Pete discovered 'e'd forgotten t'bring 'is mouthpiece.

MARGARET: 'Ow annoying. But wot about the sign you were mentioning, Mr. Gill?

GILL: Well like A sez, "Send an 'and t'grasp me foot like". Then A must 'a' dropped off.

MARGARET: Y' fell asleep did y'?

GILL: Aye. When A woke up it woh light. A cud see t'sky through a chink in t'curtains. It woh blue wi' some white clouds

MARGARET: But wot about this sign then?

GILL: A wor 'oldin' me own foot in me own 'and.

MARGARET: When you woke up?

GILL: Aye.

MARGARET: An' that was wot you interpreted really as a sort of sign cummin' from the er Lord?

GILL: Aye. A'd been to Elland

MARGARET: Yes, A know. It was the sign that made you start sellin', was it?

GILL: Well. A mean. 'E'd indicated 'Is existence like. The' must be sum purpose. A waited like t' 'ear wot it was. A wor in a record shop. List'nin' t'a Monk LP. It 'ad Liza on one side an'

MARGARET: But wot 'er transpired as y' were listenin'?

GILL: An urge like. It cum t'me. Relinquish. Embrace poverty. Sell foh God like.

(LINDA *sits up.*)

LINDA: Y're nuts. Crackers. Sell foh God. Ugh. Y're round t'bend.

MARGARET: Ah, Linda, are y' feelin' better now?

LINDA: A shan't feel better till 'e's gone. Clear off. Go on.

MARGARET: Mr. Gill will leave in a minute now just when A've 'ad a chance t'buy sumthing off 'im.

LINDA: Y're not going t' buy owt?

MARGARET: It is for charity after all.

LINDA: A don't believe it. 'E gives me t'creeps. Get out. Go on. Go on.

79

MARGARET: Now, Linda

LINDA: 'O's side a' you on?

MARGARET: A'm not takin' sides. Now, Mr. Gill, please tell me
wot A can purchase for a good cause.

(GILL *fumbles in the case. Holds up an old worn toothbrush.*)

LINDA: Ugh. No. Sumd'y's mucky toothbrush. 'Is! N-no. A'll
be sick. Aah, Aah. N-no. N-no. N-no. N-no. N-no.

(*She collapses in hysterics into a chair. Huddles sobbing.*)

MARGARET: Oh dear. 'Ow much, Mr. Gill, please?

GILL: Fourpence.

(*She hands him fourpence from her trousers' pocket.*)

MARGARET: Thank you.

GILL: Ta. Thanks. Bless y'.

(*He takes an old purse from somewhere. It is empty until he
puts the fourpence into it.*)

MARGARET: Thank you a lot, Mr. Gill, but now A'm sorry but
y'll 'ave t' be on y'r way doin' the Lord's work.

(*She closes his case for him.*)

GILL: Thanks. A will. God bless y', Missis.

(*She leads him gently to the door.*)

MARGARET: That's all right, Mr. Gill.

GILL: Bless y'. Aye, bless y'.

MARGARET: Thank you, Mr. Gill, and the same t'you.

(*She opens the door.*)

Good-bye, Mr. Gill.

GILL: Good-bye. Thank you. Bless y'.

MARGARET: Good-bye.

(*He disappears. With an air of superior benevolence, she
watches him go down the street. She shakes her head. Then
she looks towards Linda, still huddled sobbing in a chair
with the same expression and again shakes her head. Then
she closes the door and walks to Linda's chair. She looks
down on her.*)

Poor Linda, it's all right now. Poor Mr. Gill has
gone.

BLACKOUT